Beautiful
Wooden Gifts
YOU CAN MAKE
in a Weekend

*Craft 20 heirloom projects and master new techniques—
from marquetry to turning and more*

ALAN & GILL BRIDGEWATER

POPULAR WOODWORKING BOOKS
CINCINNATI, OHIO

Read This Important Safety Notice

To prevent accidents, keep safety in mind while you work. Use the safety guards installed on power equipment; they are for your protection. When working on power equipment, keep fingers away from saw blades, wear safety goggles to prevent injuries from flying wood chips and sawdust, wear headphones to protect your hearing, and consider installing a dust vacuum to reduce the amount of airborne sawdust in your woodshop. Don't wear loose clothing, such as neckties or shirts with loose sleeves, or jewelry, such as rings, necklaces or bracelets, when working on power equipment, and tie back long hair to prevent it from getting caught in your equipment. The author and editors who compiled this book have tried to make the contents as accurate and correct as possible. Plans, illustrations, photographs and text have been carefully checked. All instructions, plans and projects should be carefully read, studied and understood before beginning construction. Due to the variability of local conditions, construction materials, skill levels, etc., neither the authors nor Popular Woodworking Books assumes any responsibility for any accidents, injuries, damages or other losses incurred resulting from the material presented in this book.

Beautiful Wooden Gifts You Can Make in a Weekend. Copyright © 1998 by Alan and Gill Bridgewater. Manufactured in China. All rights reserved. No part of this book may be reproduced in any form or by any electronic or mechanical means including information storage and retrieval systems without permission in writing from the publisher, except by a reviewer, who may quote brief passages in a review. Published by Popular Woodworking Books, an imprint of F&W Publications, Inc., 1507 Dana Avenue, Cincinnati, Ohio 45207. (800) 289-0963. First edition.

This hardcover edition of *Beautiful Wooden Gifts You Can Make in a Weekend* features a "self-jacket" that eliminates the need for a separate dust jacket. It provides sturdy protection for your book while it saves paper, trees and energy.

Other fine Popular Woodworking Books are available from your local bookstore or direct from the publisher.

02 01 00 99 98   5 4 3 2 1

Library of Congress Cataloging-in-Publication Data

Bridgewater, Alan.
   Beautiful wooden gifts you can make in a weekend / by Alan and Gill Bridgewater.—1st ed.
       p.   cm.
   Includes bibliographical references and index.
   ISBN 1-55870-452-3 (alk. paper)
   1. Woodwork. 2. House furnishings. I. Bridgewater, Gill. II. Title.
TT180.B75 1998
684'.08—dc21   97-34530
                                 CIP

Edited by Bruce Stoker
Production edited by Jennifer Lepore
Interior designed by Kathleen DeZarn
Cover designed by Brian Roeth

METRIC CONVERSION CHART

TO CONVERT	TO	MULTIPLY BY
Inches	Centimeters	2.54
Centimeters	Inches	0.4
Feet	Centimeters	30.5
Centimeters	Feet	0.03
Yards	Meters	0.9
Meters	Yards	1.1
Sq. Inches	Sq. Centimeters	6.45
Sq. Centimeters	Sq. Inches	0.16
Sq. Feet	Sq. Meters	0.09
Sq. Meters	Sq. Feet	10.8
Sq. Yards	Sq. Meters	0.8
Sq. Meters	Sq. Yards	1.2
Pounds	Kilograms	0.45
Kilograms	Pounds	2.2
Ounces	Grams	28.4
Grams	Ounces	0.04

DEDICATION

We would like to dedicate this book to Peter and Lorraine—over the years they have given us a huge amount of help and advice.

ACKNOWLEDGMENTS

We would also like to thank the manufacturers who have supplied us with the best of the best . . .

Tim Effrem, President, Wood Carvers Supply
P.O. Box 7500
Englewood, FL 34295-7500
Woodcarving Tools

Jim Brewer, Research and Marketing Manager, Freud
P.O. Box 7187
218 Feld Ave.
High Point, NC 27264
Forstner Drill Bits

John P. Jodkin, Vice President, Delta International
    Machinery Corp.
246 Alpha Dr.
Pittsburgh, PA 15238-2985
Band Saw

Dawn Fretz, Marketing Assistant, De-Sta-Co
P.O. Box 2800
Troy, MI 48007
Clamps

Paragon Communications, Evo-Stick
Common Rd.
Stafford, ST16 3EH, UK
PVA Adhesive

Frank Cootz, Public Relations, Ryobi America Corp.
5201 Pearman Dairy Rd., Suite 1
P.O. Box 1207
Anderson, SC 29622-1207
Thickness Planner

Glen Tizzard, Draper Tools UK
Hursley Rd., Chandlers Ford
Eastleigh, Hampshire SO5 5YF UK
Scroll Saw

Legno Ltd.
35 Leyton Industrial Village, Argall Ave.
Leyton, London E10 7QP
Veneers

Last but not least, we would like to thank Angelo Giovino, Matt Haycock, Kevin Hutson and Glyn Bridgewater for their woodworking help.

TABLE OF CONTENTS

TEDDY BEAR BANK
8

TURNED AND PIERCED
POTPOURRI BOX
12

DUCK DECOY
30

MATCHING LETTER OPENER
AND DESK SET
35

MINIATURE MANTLE CLOCK
27

HEART-SHAPED CHEESE BOARD
17

CLASSIC BOW SAW
43

CARVED FRUIT BOWL
49

LAMINATED KEEPSAKE BOX
22

GILDED SCROLL SHELF
54

HEART-SHAPED PUZZLE BOX
62

TRADITIONAL
SPRINGERLE
BOARD
67

OLD-FASHIONED PUSH-ALONG TOYS
94

TURNED SALT AND PEPPER MILLS
101

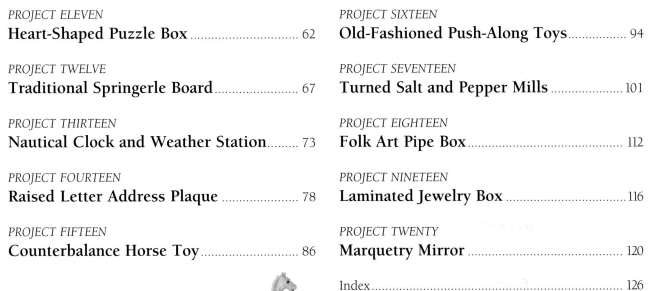

NAUTICAL CLOCK AND WEATHER STATION
73

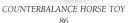

RAISED LETTER ADDRESS PLAQUE
78

COUNTERBALANCE HORSE TOY
86

FOLK ART
PIPE BOX
112

MARQUETRY MIRROR
120

LAMINATED
JEWELRY BOX
116

INTRODUCTION

Wood is beautiful! Wood never ceases to beguile me. Wood has unique qualities—it is strong, it flexes, it twists, it is aromatic, it has color and texture, and it can last a lifetime.

I love everything about wood, its form, the way it feels, the way it can be sawed, the way it can be pared with a chisel, the way it can be planed. I am bewitched by every aspect of its ever-changing character.

And I'm not the only one who is obsessing over wood—it has always been thus. In fact, in countries and areas as far apart in time and space as pre-industrial Europe, the Northwest coast of North America, in nineteenth-century Asia, in Africa, in India, and just about all over, wood was considered to be so extraordinary that it was deemed sacred. This feeling that wood and trees were somehow special was often expressed in terms of making the wood into traditional objects—masks, boxes, weapons, images—and then presenting the items as gifts. So, for example, in rural pre-industrial Europe, the moment some poor love-lorn lad found a sweetheart he would take a sharp knife and a carefully selected piece of wood, and start whittling a love token. He might carve a heart-shaped box, a puzzle chain or a corset stiffener and then go on to decorate it with plump twined hearts, initials, flowers and so on. The feeling behind a love token was that not only would it last forever—like the love—but that the effort and energy put into the carving would somehow transform, or you might say, bless, the wood.

And so it was, in many countries and cultures, that wood was turned into gifts considered to have a unique significance and value. The wonderful thing is that here I am, in the last years of the twentieth century, extolling the fact that wood is more significant, more precious and more meaningful than ever. My message to you is that a gift made from wood, a gift you have shaped and crafted, is so very different from a gift purchased pre-packaged and ready-made that it is in many ways truly unique!

It has been said that a gift made from wood is twice blessed—it blesses the maker and it blesses the receiver. Certainly, there is no doubting a gift made from wood provides a challenge that, allied to its beauty and unpredictability, makes it singular.

When we first sat down to figure out the projects in this book, we were overwhelmed with ideas—there were so many wonderful things we could make, that it was something of a problem. And then it came to us: Not only did the "unique gifts" need to be small—there is, after all, something special about a wooden item that can easily be picked up in one hand—but more than that, they needed to be carefully targeted. As we saw it, woodworkers would sooner or later feel the need to make gifts for all their friends and family. I'm sure you know what I mean—gifts for sons and daughters, mom and dad, brothers and sisters, granny and granddad, aunts and uncles, the kids next door and the couple across the road. And as you can see, we have included gifts for all. If you want to make a gift for your boss, your wife, your husband, the kids or whomever, all are catered to.

So there you have it; you are going to enjoy this book. With each and every project, we take you through all the steps. There are black-and-white shots that describe the step-by-step stages, line drawings that describe difficult details, special tips, and all manner of discussions and asides to help you in your quest. As for the working drawings, we have even gone to the trouble of painstakingly drawing the run and character of the grain so you can see at a glance how the side, face and end grain areas relate to one another. In fact, we have done our level best to see to it that you have a grand time with the wood, chisels and planes . . . beautiful!

What else to say except that the pity of it is, once you have made the projects, you have to give them away! Or do you?

Teddy Bear Bank

W hen I was a kid about six years old or so, I was obsessed with money! Or as my brothers would have said—still say—I was a "Mr. Mean," a scrooge, a tightwad, a hoarder, a miser. Whenever my relatives came around for a visit, I would smile and give kisses, and generally do all the things most kids of that age hate to do, in the hope that my oh-so-wonderful behavior would put me in line for a monetary handout.

It rarely failed! When the moment came to say good-bye, my sycophantic behavior usually paid off, with my doting uncles and aunts vying with each other to give me all their loose change. The funny thing was, I didn't really care about the money as such, I simply enjoyed putting coins in my automated money box!

This project draws its inspiration from my long-gone toy—when the lever is pushed down, it causes the coin to fall through the slot, and causes the bear to raise his arm and nod his head.

MAKING THE TEDDY BEAR BANK

Having studied the working drawings for making the box and carefully selected your wood, set out the various dimensions and cut out the ten component parts—the four sides, the base, the top and the four inside-corner fillets. Cut the rabbets at the corners and glue up. Round over the edges of the base and lid with a quarter-curve profile and fit with countersunk screws.

Trace the side-view profile of the bear through to your chosen wood—best if it's a soft easy-to-carve timber like lime, jelutong or basswood—and cut it out on the scroll saw. Rerun this procedure for the front views. You should finish up with six parts—the head, the body, two arms

PROJECT ONE: WORKING DRAWING

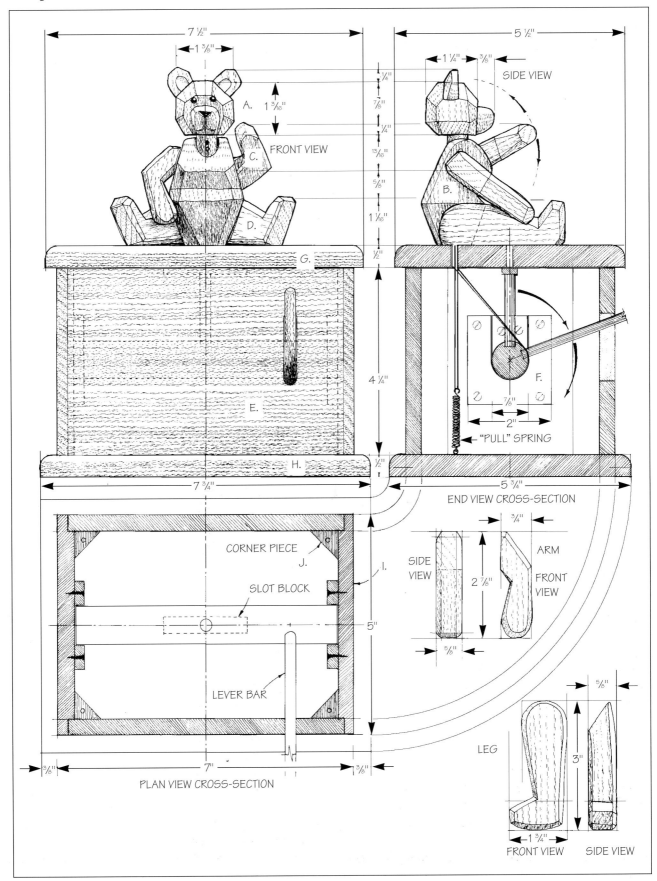

7 ½"

1 ³⁄₈"

A.   1 ³⁄₁₆"

FRONT VIEW

C.

D.

G.

E.

H.

7 ¾"

CORNER PIECE

J.

SLOT BLOCK

LEVER BAR

7"

³⁄₈"   ³⁄₈"

PLAN VIEW CROSS-SECTION

5 ½"

1 ¼"   ³⁄₈"

SIDE VIEW

¼"

⅞"

¼"

13⁄16"

⅝"

1 1⁄16"

½"

4 ¼"

½"

B.

F.

⅞"

2"

"PULL" SPRING

END VIEW CROSS-SECTION

5 ¾"

I.

5"

SIDE VIEW

2 ⅞"

⅝"

³⁄₄"

ARM

FRONT VIEW

LEG

³⁄₈"

5⁄16"

3"

1 ³⁄₄"

FRONT VIEW   SIDE VIEW

and two legs. Drill ½″-diameter holes down through the body, up into the head, through the shoulder and into the arm, and fit stubs of ½″-dowel for the neck and for the jointed arm.

When you have made the basic parts for the bear, use a knife to swiftly whittle the cutouts to shape. Don't try for anything fancy, just go for uncomplicated and stylized chunky forms.

Finally, having first used a scalpel and sandpaper to tidy up and create a good finish, use a dash of black acrylic paint to detail the nose, eyes and mouth.

PUTTING IT TOGETHER

Once you have made the box and all the parts that go to make the bear, then comes the difficult task of putting the whole thing together. It's not so much that any single stage is difficult, but that everything has got to be just right. If one of the control strings is too slack, or the shaft is too tight, or whatever, then the movement won't work.

Start by running 1⁄16″-diameter holes through the neck and arm stubs. The neck needs a side-to-side hole for the pivot and a front-to-back hole for the control cords, while the arm needs a single front-to-back through-hole for both the control cords and the pivot strings. In essence, the controls are beautifully simple. There are four cords—one to pull the head down, one to pull the head up, one to pull the arm down and one to pull the arm up. And of course, depending upon how you want the action to go, fix either the "up" or the "down" cords to a lightweight tension "pulling" spring so the lever action becomes the positive movement.

Finally, when you are happy with the movement, cut two slots in the box (one for the lever and one for the coins), fit the shaft with its dowels and end plates, glue-fix the bear to the top of the box, run the control cords down into the box and then variously tie the cords to the spring or shaft.

MATERIALS LIST—PROJECT ONE

TEDDY BEAR

A Head (1)	2″×2″×2″
B Body (1)	2″×2″×3″
C Arms (2)	1″×¾″×3″
D Legs (2)	¾″×2″×3″

Note that all the above pieces are oversize and allow for cutting waste.

BOX

E Front (2)	3″×4¼″×6½″
F Shaft plates (2)	¼″×2″×2″
G Top (1)	½″×5½″×7½″
H Bottom (1)	½″×5¾″×7¾″
I End (2)	⅜″×5″×4¼″
J Corner fillets (4)	⅝″ triangular section at 4½″ long

HARDWARE AND EXTRAS

K Drive shaft (1) broomstick dowel—cut to fit
L Slot and lever bars (2) ¼″ dowel—cut to fit
M Strong cord—to fit
N Brass screws—various
O Small quantity of black acrylic paint

Note that all box measurements are to size.

SPECIAL TIP: GLUING

For swiftly fitting and fixing all the control cords, you can't do better than a cyanoacrylate. It's good for holding the knots tight, for little trial-and-error holds, for fixing the bear to the top of the box. In fact, it's just about perfect for everything.

STEP-BY-STEP STAGES

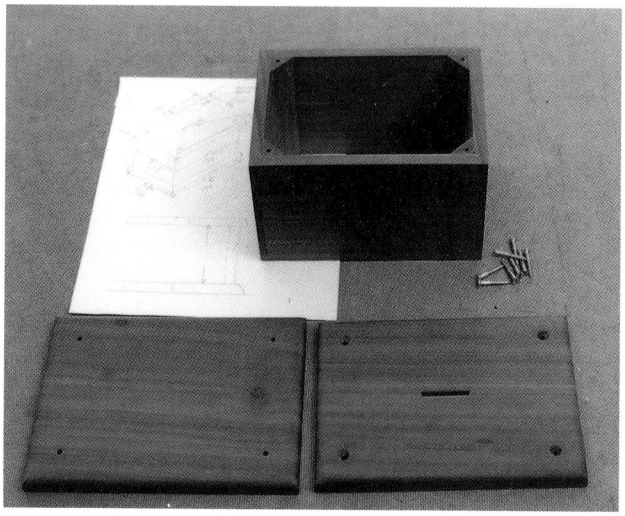

1 The finished box, with the bottom and top slabs ready to fit. Note how the fixing screws are placed so they run into the corner fillets.

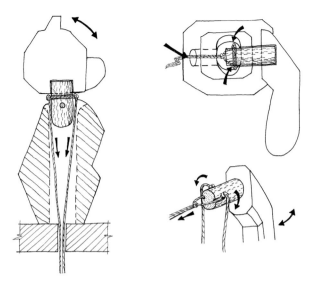

2 Next we string the bear. This cross section shows how the control cords operate the up-and-down movement of the head on the pivot. Be sure to use strong twine and nonslip knots. Notice the plan view at top right, showing how the arm is both pivoted and controlled by the cords. A detail of the cord is shown at bottom right. See how one cord pulls and pivots the arm, while the other two cords operate the up-and-down movement.

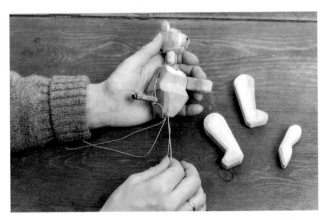

3 Have a dry run before you start gluing and fixing. Notice how I have left plenty of length to the cords.

SPECIAL TIP: MODELS

If you can't figure out how the movement works, make a working model with a card, pins and rubber bands. Make a card cutout of a bear, fix it to a board with thumbtacks at the joints, and then run cords from the various limbs in such a way that a pull-down on the cord results in the limb flipping up. If you now have rubber bands to pull the limbs back into the original position, then you have achieved an archetypal string-and-spring movement.

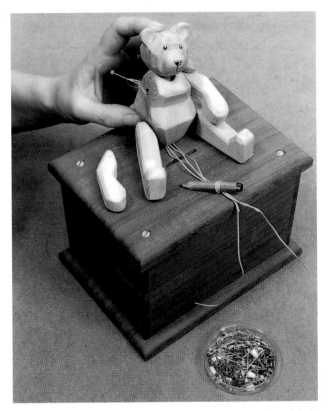

4 Sit the bear in place on top of the box and establish the position of the cord hole. If necessary, sand the various mating faces of the limbs and the body, so as to adjust the pose.

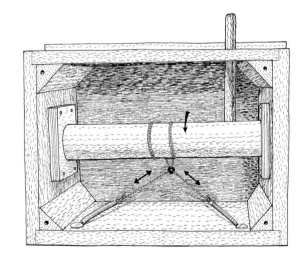

5 A view into the underside of the box shows the fixing of the four cords. One cord each from the arm and the head run down to the springs, while the other two cords are wrapped and glued around the shaft. In action, the lever turns the shaft, with the effect that the strings pull down on the arm and head.

Turned and Pierced Potpourri Box

Wood turning, cutting delicate frets with a scroll saw, and whittling are three of my favorite woodworking activities. The problem, when I first started thinking about this project, was how could I incorporate the three techniques to create a single unique item? After a good deal of thought I came up with the notion for this project—a turned box with a pierced lid, with a small amount of knife work in and around the piercing.

The design draws its inspiration from two of my friends, one a wood turner and the other a general woodworker. However, they both needed a fresh angle to spark off their talents. Well, to cut a long story short, Gill came up with this great idea that they combine their talents so as to halve their workshop expenses and double their money-making potential. The good news is that they now make the most beautiful turned and pierced containers, and they are both scooping up the rewards!

TURNING THE BOX

Though there are any number of ways of turning a small lidded box of this type and character, the best way is to use the four-jaw chuck technique. The procedure is wonderfully simple and direct. Having mounted the wood in the chuck, you start by turning the wood down to a 4″-diameter cylinder, and parting off the tailstock end of the cylinder for the lid. This done, you hollow turn the box and cut the step on the rim, then take the surface to a good finish and part off.

The next step is perhaps slightly tricky. You remount the lid section on the lathe and start by hollowing out the

PROJECT TWO: WORKING DRAWING

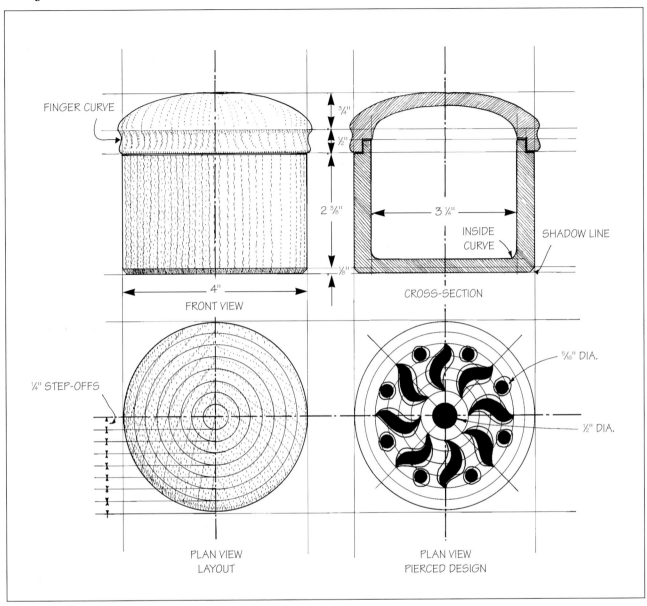

FINGER CURVE

¾"

½"

2 ⅜"

⅛"

4"

FRONT VIEW

3 ¼"

INSIDE CURVE

SHADOW LINE

CROSS-SECTION

¼" STEP-OFFS

PLAN VIEW LAYOUT

⁵⁄₁₆" DIA.

½" DIA.

PLAN VIEW PIERCED DESIGN

lid and cutting the rim to fit the base. Then you remove the lid from the chuck, turn it over so that the expanding jaws of the chuck fit the inside of the rim, and finish up by turning the top of the lid. Don't forget to set the lid out with the ¼" step-off lines to help later when you set out the design.

SPECIAL TIP: SCROLL SAW LIMITS

If you like the idea of this project but are planning to change the shape of the turned box, or even change the placing of the pierced holes, be mindful that the overall design is more or less governed by the use of the electric scroll saw. For example: As the saw is unable to cut wood thicker than about 1¾", the lid can't be high and/or domed. Also, the saw can't be used to fret a pierced design

around the box.

All that said, if you are keen to change the pierced design and/or the shape of the lid, you could possibly use a jeweler's piercing saw or perhaps a fine-blade hand fretsaw. It needs a bit of thinking about.

FRETTING, PIERCING AND WHITTLING THE LID

When you have made the turned box, with the lid nicely set out with the ¼" guidelines, it's time to fret out the design. Pencil-press transfer the design through to the wood, bore out round holes with appropriate size bits, drill small pilot holes through the "windows" of the design, and fret out the shapes on the scroll saw. Finally, use the point of the knife to trim back the sharp edges of the piercings.

STEP-BY-STEP STAGES

1 When you have sanded and smoothed the lid to a good finish, use the point of the skew chisel to set the lid out with a series of rings. Space them about ¼″ apart. The idea is that you can use them as a guide to lay out the design.

2 Shade in the pierced areas so that there is no doubt about the line of cut. If you are worried about the pencil smudging, then it's a good idea to give the whole lid a quick spray with pencil fixative as used by illustrators.

MATERIALS LIST—PROJECT TWO

A Board (1)   4½″ × 4½″ × 6″

Note: Because we were a bit short of wood, we decided to laminate two pieces to make the 4½″ × 4½″ × 6″ section.

3 It's most important that you use Forstner bits for the large holes that make up the design. I say this because they are the only bit types that guarantee perfect-every-time holes.

4 Take two cuts for each end of the little curved shape. Work from the central pilot hole and down toward the point so that the point is crisp and sharp.

USING THE LATHE AND THE FOUR-JAW CHUCK

Though wood turning is one of the most important woodworking activities—vital for making just about everything from chair legs, stair balustrades, and bedposts, to boxes, candlesticks and bowls—it is also one of the most misunderstood of all the woodworking techniques. What happens with most beginners is that they purchase an "amateur" machine and a set of "starter" tools, and then become disenchanted when they can't make anything more exciting than small spindles. The problem, of course, is that small machines tend to wobble and shake, and the pronged center and the fixed tailstock center that are supplied with most small machines are totally inadequate and almost useless. As a result, many beginners soon get disillusioned and decide to give up wood turning. The pity of it is that the majority of these disillusioned beginners heap blame on themselves. Of course, what these beginners simply can't know is that turning is the one area of woodworking where the old adage "a poor workman always blames his tools" is a load of bunk! In the context of wood turning, the boring old adage ought more rightly read "poor results are nearly *always* the result of poor tools." All this adds up to the inescapable fact that exciting and varied wood turning can only really be achieved if you have top quality tools and equipment.

So there you go. If you are a beginner looking to get started, the following pointers will show you the way.

Lathe

In essence, a lathe is a woodworking machine used for cutting and shaping wood into a round section. The wood is pivoted and spun between centers and/or held in a chuck, while at the same time handheld chisels or gouges are used to make the cuts. Though there are many lathe types—small ones, large ones, very long ones, some dedicated to making spindles, some dedicated to making bowls, some with fancy multispeed controls, and so on— experience tells me that a large traditional lathe, with a big motor and a heavy cast-iron frame, is by far the best option. I say this because while a miniature lathe might well be superb for making small items like lace bobbins, it can't be used to make larger pieces like bowls and chair legs. A large lathe, on the other hand, can be used to make everything from lace bobbins to bedposts. As for the cast-iron frame of a large lathe, there's no rust, no vibration, no nothing—it just sits there and does the job! I have a large old English lathe called a Harrison Jubilee, made about 1940. It is a wonderful machine.

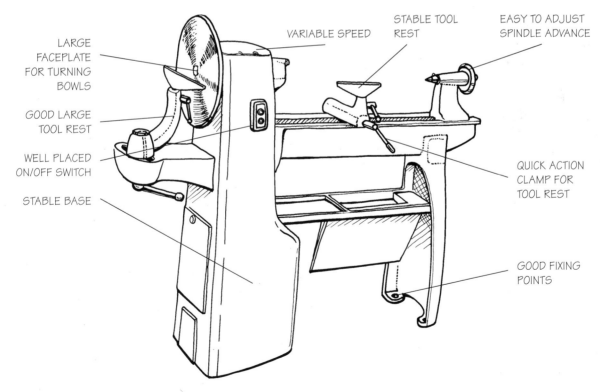

LARGE FACEPLATE FOR TURNING BOWLS

GOOD LARGE TOOL REST

WELL PLACED ON/OFF SWITCH

STABLE BASE

VARIABLE SPEED

STABLE TOOL REST

EASY TO ADJUST SPINDLE ADVANCE

QUICK ACTION CLAMP FOR TOOL REST

GOOD FIXING POINTS

LATHE ANATOMY
If the notion of wood turning appeals to you, then be sure to invest in the biggest, best quality lathe that you can afford.

HEADSTOCK AND TAILSTOCK

The headstock, the power-driven unit at the left-hand side of the lathe, carries the bearings in which the spindle revolves. The spindle has an external screw for chucks and faceplates and an internal taper for the pronged center. The tailstock, the movable unit at the right-hand side of the lathe, holds a pointed center. The distance between the headstock and the tailstock can be adjusted by winding the tailstock center in or out.

TOOL REST

The tool rest, sometimes called T-rest, is the unit that moves left or right along the bed on which the tools—meaning the gouges and chisels—are rested. Being mindful that the rest is a fulcrum for the levering action of the tools, it is essential that it can be swiftly and easily moved and put in place.

THE BED

The bed is the metal track, rods or rails that link the headstock to the tailstock, upon which the tool rest slides. Since it is vital that you are able to swiftly and easily move the tool rest, it is best to avoid narrow-slot, round-section bar beds that easily get clogged up with dust and shavings.

Four-Jaw Chuck

The four-jaw chuck is a mechanism used to hold the workpiece; it is a device that replaces the pronged center and all manner of other centers. Operated by a chuck key, the four jaws can be opened and closed in unison in such a way that they grip square sections. To my way of thinking the four-jaw chuck is essential. Okay, so four-jaw chucks are expensive—mine cost one-quarter the price of my secondhand lathe—and they do need to be fitted with a guard. But they grip wood without the need to turn it down to a round section—a huge time-saver—and once the wood is in the chuck, you can be confident that it's going to stay put.

When I said at the beginning that you can make just about everything you care to imagine on a large lathe, I should really have added the proviso: but only if you use a four-jaw chuck. You should see me at my lathe. I don't mess around with pronged centers or faceplates. I threw them away long since. I simply mount everything on the four-jaw chuck and get straight into the job. As well as holding square sections without the need for preparation, the jaws are good for other uses, such as holding rings and containers, holding a large screw—instead of using a screw center—and gripping round sections.

FOUR-JAW CHUCK
The advantage of the four-jaw chuck is that you can draw the tailstock center out of the way and approach the workpiece head-on.

Heart-Shaped Cheese Board

This project had its beginnings in our ever-pressing need to tidy up our workshop. The problem was, of course, what to do with the mountain of offcuts? I'm sure you know what I mean. The chair, table, box or whatever is finished, and you are left with great heaps of wood. Okay, maybe the longer lengths can be used for the next job in line, and the shavings can be used as fuel or as bedding for your chickens, and the dust can be swept up and put in the trash, but what to do with the medium-size bits and pieces that look too good to throw away?

Well, after a deal of thought, we came up with the super-brilliant idea of cutting all our small offcuts down to a uniform size, and then laminating the resultant blocks to make cutting boards and surfaces that needed to show end grain. Okay, so it is a solution that involves a lot of time, sweat and effort, but then again, the finished boards can be presented or marketed as choice handcrafted items.

So there you go. If you are up to your knees in offcuts, or you are short of cash and maybe know of a sawmill operator who is looking to give away his trimmings free, then perhaps this is the project for you!

PROJECT THREE: WORKING DRAWING

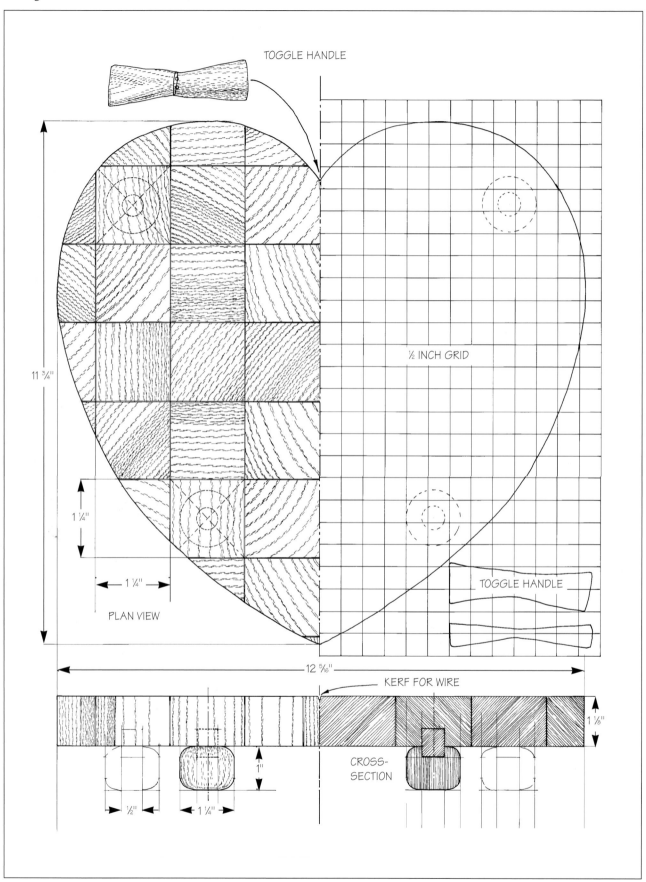

TOGGLE HANDLE

½ INCH GRID

TOGGLE HANDLE

11 ¾"

1 ¼"

1 ¼"

PLAN VIEW

12 ⁵⁄₁₆"

KERF FOR WIRE

1 ⅛"

CROSS-
SECTION

1"

½"

1 ¼"

MAKING THE BOARD

Collect all your waste wood and cut it down to the best overall section size. I went for a square section 1¾″×1¾″, but you can just as well go for 1″×1″ or 1″×1½″, or whatever size best suits your material. And, of course, if you want to use a mix of sizes, then no matter, as long as the grain is running along the length and the corners are true at 90°. Having achieved your sawed size, plane the wood down to a smooth finish. When you are happy with the finish, saw it down to 1⅛″ slices. When you have a stockpile of 1⅛″ slices, pencil label the end-grain face, arrange the slices side by side in rows of about 12″ long, and spend time working out how best to clamp them together. You can use a couple of G-clamps and a bar clamp, or a jig and wedges; no matter, as long as the arrangement is such that you can apply end pressure without the strips bending or bowing along their length.

Do the gluing-up in two stages: first the blocks side by side to make the strips, and then the strips side by side to make the slabs. Draw the design of the board on the slab, cut out the profile and sand the end-grain surfaces to a good finish. Fit the whittled feet and the cutting wire, give the whole works a coat of matte varnish and the project is finished.

SPECIAL TIP: DRY FIT FIRST

As the success of this project hinges on your being able to glue and clamp dozens of the little blocks together, it is important that you plan out the procedure. The best way is to have a trial dry run, with everything in place except the glue. You need to check out the glue type and make sure that it's suitable, clear an area and make sure that there is room to maneuver, have cloths and newspaper handy, and so on. And then you have to actually clamp-up the wood and see how your arrangement works out. Okay, so maybe my way of working does sound a bit fussy, but the horrible alternative is to have glue smeared all over the place, only to find that the clamp isn't long enough, or you have glued the wrong surfaces, or you are missing some vital piece of equipment.

STEP-BY-STEP STAGES

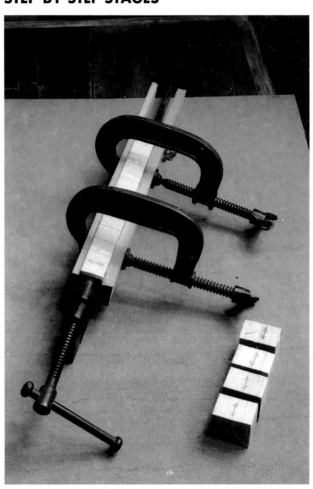

1 Saw the 1¾″×1¾″ square section of wood down into 1⅛″ thick slices—like slices off a loaf of bread—and then clamp up. With the arrows indicating the run of the grain, you can see how the slices of wood need to be realigned when it comes to gluing.

MATERIALS LIST—PROJECT THREE

A Board	1¾″×1¾″ offcuts—enough to suit the size of your board
B Feet (1)	1½″×½″×6″ ½″ dowel × 4″ long
C Toggle handle (1)	fancy hardwood ½″×1″×4″

HARDWARE AND EXTRAS

D Cheese wire (1)	15″ long

Note that all measurements allow for a small amount of cutting waste.

4 Having whittled a small piece of hardwood to a butterfly shape and sanded it to a super smooth finish, run two side-by-side $\frac{1}{16}''$-diameter holes through the center of the bow, and knot the wire in place.

2 The best way of ensuring that the little ball feet stay in keeping with the total design is to whittle them to shape. I drilled and doweled four little square blocks, cut the corners off the blocks to make rough octagonals, and used a largish sloyd knife for the whittling.

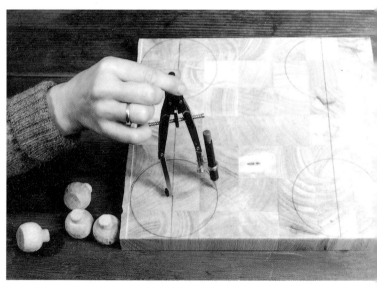

5 And just in case you have an aversion to heart shapes, there is no reason at all why you can't go for just about any shape that takes your fancy. For example, you can simply round the corners of a rectangular board.

3 To fix the wire, drill a $\frac{1}{8}''$-diameter hole, set the wire in the hole and then follow it up with a glued dowel. Make a saw cut between the cheeks, wrap the wire over and around in the cut and follow it up with a glued sliver wedge.

DEBRIS COLLECTION AND WOODSHOP SAFETY

Woodshop debris, in the form of offcuts, shavings and sawdust scattered around on the floor and over the surfaces, is a dangerous nuisance. The shavings make the floor slippery and the loose offcuts are potential ankle-breakers. And of course, the wood dust not only clogs the machines, it is a fire risk, it creeps into the home, and it also harms the lungs.

Just how much dust is considered to be dangerous? The Occupational Safety and Health Administration (OSHA) suggests that if you can see wood dust floating around in the atmosphere when a shaft of sunlight shines across the workshop, then you have a problem that needs solving.

We tackle the problem in several ways: We cut the amount of dust down at the source by using filtered machines and by producing shavings rather than dust, and we have a large mobile vacuum system that we move around to service the various machines. We also wear a rubber dust/vapor mask for most tasks—like sawing, drilling, and when we are using varnish and such—and a full-face electric visor-helmet respirator when we are working at the lathe. As to which mask does the better job, the rubber mask is silent but uncomfortable and sweaty, while the electric full-face respirator is a bit heavy and noisy.

In the context of sawdust being bad for your lungs, I reckon that tried-and-trusted traditional American and European woods like ash, oak, beech, maple, willow, pear and pine are generally much safer than exotic species such as mahogany, obeche and iroko. All that said, if you find yourself sneezing, or your nose is running, or your skin develops a rash, then you best go for another wood type.

So what to do if you are really worried about dust and allergic reactions and such? Well, I think that for safety's sake, you need to stay with the following rules of thumb:

■ Whenever possible use hand tool techniques that produce shavings rather than dust.

■ Use traditional white-wood species that are non-oily to the touch.

■ Use a vacuum machine to suck up the dust as it is produced—before it gets a chance to puff around the workshop.

■ Wear a full-face mask, and always wash your hands and face after work.

■ Always have a thorough sweep-up at the end of the day.

■ If you have a health problem, then ask the advice of your doctor.

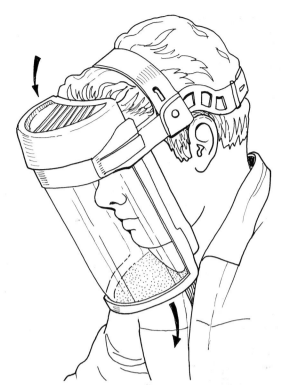

ELECTRIC VISOR-HELMET RESPIRATOR
Though the choice of mask does in many ways depend upon your personal preference—they both have their plus points—I usually wear the full-face respirator when I am working at the lathe, for the plain, simple reason that the full-face visor offers additional protection from flying debris.

Laminated Keepsake Box

Though you might think that a box is a box is a box and not very exciting, this particular little box is rather special. Not only does it use wood that might otherwise be thrown away, but better yet, the layering technique allows you to very easily modify the length, width and height to suit your own needs. You could call it a "log cabin" box. This refers to the way the sections are layered one on top of another with the ends staggered, just the way the old timers built their log cabins.

MAKING THE BOX

When you have studied the working drawings and seen how the lid and the base boards are set into slots—with the lid being able to slide in and out—then make decisions as to the size of your box, and size and plane the wood accordingly.

If you are going to stay with our design, you need twenty-four $\frac{1}{2}''\times\frac{1}{2}''$-square sections in all, twelve long and twelve short. All I did was search through my pile of offcuts, select two colors that went together to make a pleasant counterchange, and then pushed the wood through my portable surface planer. Having planed the wood to a crisp $\frac{1}{2}''\times\frac{1}{2}''$-square section, cut the wood to length so that it is perfectly square-ended and slightly oversize. As the long pieces need to end up at $5\frac{1}{2}''$—meaning when they are built into the finished $6''$-long box—it's best to cut them at about $5\frac{5}{8}''$, so you can plane and sand them back to a good fit and finish.

When you have made the twenty-four lengths, pile them up in a dry-run arrangement, in the order they are going to be in the finished box, and pencil mark the top and bottom layers of the stack. Draw in registration marks

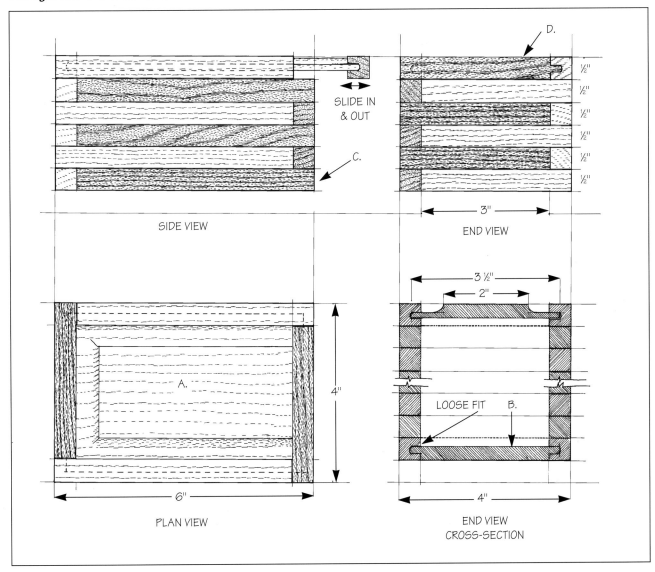

SLIDE IN
& OUT

C.

SIDE VIEW

D.

½"
½"
½"
½"
½"
½"

3"

END VIEW

A.

4"

6"

PLAN VIEW

3 ½"

2"

LOOSE FIT   B.

4"

END VIEW
CROSS-SECTION

so there is no doubting the layered order.

Being very careful that you don't make a mistake, take the eight lengths that go to make the top and the bottom layers and use either a router or a grooving plane to cut the channels. Aim to have the grooves at about 3/16″ wide, ¼″ deep, and centered in the ½″ thickness of the wood.

With the channels crisply worked, take the wood that you have chosen for the base and the lid and use a router or a plane to cut the rabbeted edges. While you are at it, use a router or a "round" moulding plane, or even a gouge, to cut the beautiful scooped convex curve that runs down from the top face of the lid through to the rabbet.

Starting at the base and working up, glue the four base lengths together so that the base board is nicely contained, and then layer up in log cabin fashion until the box is complete. Don't forget to leave one of the top-end pieces

unglued. This done, test to make sure that the lid is a good fit and leave the box until the glue is set. Glue the short length on the end of the lid board.

Finally, plane and sand the box down to a flush-sided smooth finish, make sure that the lid is a nice easy fit in the grooves, and then wax and burnish to a high sheen.

MATERIALS LIST—PROJECT FOUR

A	Lid (1)	3/8″ × 3½″ × 5½″
B	Base (1)	3/8″ × 3½″ × 5½″
C	Long lengths (12)	½″ × ½″ × 5⅝″
D	Short lengths (12)	½″ × ½″ × 3⅝″

SPECIAL TIP: USING OLD PLANES

Though there are any number of ways of cutting tongues, grooves and rabbets, I think that the old metal grooving plane takes a bit of beating, meaning one of the old metal Stanley or Record planes. I use a Record 043 and 044, both made sometime before 1950. It's true they are no longer made, but I picked mine up at a flea market for no more than the cost of a new router bit. The Record 044 has eight blades that range in size from 1/8″ to 9/16″.

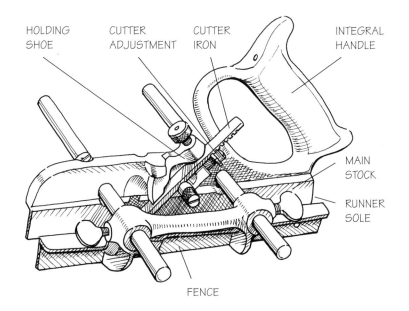

USING OLD PLANES

The classic Record 044 grooving plane is a beauty, easy to tune and pretty foolproof to use.

STEP-BY-STEP STAGES

1 With the base dry fitted in place—meaning no glue—layer the square sections up log-cabin style so that the ends stick out beyond the corners. Pay particular attention to the alignment of the grooves.

2 When you are happy with the overall shape and alignment of the box, use a ruler and square to check for squareness.

3 Before you leave the glue to set, make sure that the lid is an easy but snug fit and that it runs right through to the end of the box, so that the end runs into the groove.

4 Cut a rabbet along the square end of the lid and fit it into the grooved end piece. When you are satisfied with the fit, then glue it in place.

5 By the time the glue has set and the whole box has moved slightly, you will almost certainly have to ease the lid and/or the groove. Make sure that the "handle" butts into the sides of the box.

6 If all is correct, the base slab should be well contained, but should fit loosely, so that the box side can move without splitting the base.

The portable surface planer is a great bench machine. All you do is feed the wood in one side, between the cutter blades and the bed, and it comes out the other side nearly finished!

PORTABLE SURFACE PLANER VS. HAND PLANES

If you are a beginner to woodworking, then sooner or later you will have to make decisions about your overall approach to the subject, or your "working philosophy." One of the main questions that you have to ask yourself is, do you want the emphasis to be on the bench power tools—meaning routers, press drills, planers and all the rest—or do you want to focus on using hand tools?

Most woodworkers I know fit in one of four groups:

- Will not use power tools at any price.
- Will grudgingly use the occasional power tool, but much prefers hand tools.
- Enjoys using power tools for most of the work, and tidies up with the hand tools.
- Very much enjoys using power tools and is reluctant to use hand tools.

I reckon that Gill and I fit into group two. We much prefer working with hand tools but will sometimes use a power tool to speed things up.

Okay, so you must surely have gathered by now, that we're not very keen on power tools. It's not so much that we can't afford to power up, but rather that we both dislike all the dust, debris and noise that power tools generate. To our way of thinking, there is nothing quite so unpleasant as being covered with fine dust and blasted with noise.

All that said, I was so tuckered out one day last summer—when I was heavily involved in the strenuous and sweat-making procedure of hand planing a massive rough-sawn oak plank—that I decided, against my better judgment, to invest in a portable planer thicknesser. To cut a long story short—or you could say to plane a fat story thinner (ha!)—when I first saw this machine, I was firmly convinced that it was the beginning of the end of my way of working. My thinking was that it would somehow or other weaken my belief that slow-and-quiet is beautiful. However, there is no denying that it has changed the way I work. For example, where I once struggled and strained with a jointer plane, and then a smoothing plane, I now pass the wood a few times through the surface planer. In fact, I have to admit that it's a beautifully efficient machine that gets a lot of use. Of course, it is noisy, and I do have to house it in its own shed, and I did have to get myself a dust sucker and a full-face respirator mask, but against that, I can now spend much more time playing around with my various grooving, moulding and combination hand planes.

Most experts would agree that the best way is to start with hand tool techniques and then power up when you fully understand your needs.

Miniature Mantle Clock

Sometimes, when I am sitting alone in my workshop, I take up one or more pieces of choice wood and feast my eyes on the various colors that make up the character of the grain. To hold the wood up to the light and see the way the grain shimmers and glows, to see how two pieces of wood look when they are held side by side—and then to imagine how the wood might be used for a special project—these are unique quality-time experiences that should not be missed.

This project draws its inspiration from one of my alone-in-the-workshop musings. The problem was how to bring together three relatively small pieces of choice exotic wood—a scrap of ebony salvaged from an old long-gone piece of furniture, a sliver of silver sycamore veneer left over from a marquetry project, and a short length of dark wood that I've been using to prop open the door. Anyway,

I tossed all sorts of ideas around in my head—a small piece of laminated jewelry? a turning? a handle for a knife? a drawer pull? And then it came to me . . . why not make a small clock case!

MAKING THE CLOCK CASE

First things first. Before you do anything else, you need to search out a miniature watch-clock and a Forstner drill bit sized to fit. For example, as my clock (described in the catalog as a "watch-clock miniature suitable for block and drilled recess mounting") measures slightly under $1^{5}/_{16}''$ diameter across the span of the back and about $^{1}/_{4}''$ in depth, I reckoned that I needed a drill size of $1^{3}/_{8}''$.

When you have obtained the clock-watch and the drill size to suit, take your chosen pieces of wood and plane and sand the mating faces down to a true finish. This

PROJECT FIVE: WORKING DRAWING

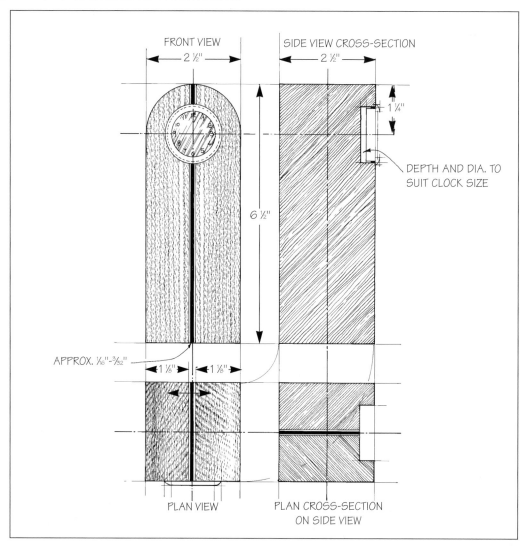

FRONT VIEW
2 ½"

SIDE VIEW CROSS-SECTION
2 ½"

1 ¼"

DEPTH AND DIA. TO
SUIT CLOCK SIZE

6 ½"

APPROX. ⅛₆"-³⁄₃₂"

1 ⅛"   1 ⅛"

PLAN VIEW

PLAN CROSS-SECTION
ON SIDE VIEW

done, smear white PVA glue on the mating faces and clamp up.

Having waited for the glue to cure, set the compass to a radius of 1¼", spike it on the center veneer at a point about 1⅜" down from top-center, and then strike off a 2½"-diameter half-circle. When you are happy with the way the lines of the design are set out on the wood, move to the band saw and cut out the curve that makes the top of the case.

Use a square to mark out the baseline, double-check that it is absolutely true, and then cut off the waste with a small-toothed backsaw. It's important that the baseline is square to the center line of the block, so spend time getting it right.

When you are sure that the block sits square and true, move to the drill press and bore out the recess for the clock. Bore down to a depth of about ⅜".

Having bored out the recess, take a scrap of sandpaper and rub down the inside of the recess, so that the clock-watch is a tight push fit. If necessary, use a straight gouge to cut a little scoop for the hand-setting knob that sticks out at the side of clock case. When you have achieved a good fit of the clock-watch in the recess, rub the whole block down on a sheet of fine-grade abrasive paper. Finally, burnish the block with beeswax, slide the clock-watch mechanism in place, and the project is finished.

SPECIAL TIP: LAPPING

The best way of rubbing the faces of the block down to a smooth, true finish is to use a technique known as lapping. All you do is mount a sheet of medium-grade abrasive paper to a slab of ½"-thick plywood so that the grit side is uppermost. Then clamp the slab in place on the bench. In use, the workpiece is rubbed in the direction of the grain, backwards and forwards. The procedure is rerun with finer and finer grades of paper.

STEP-BY-STEP STAGES

MATERIALS LIST—PROJECT FIVE

A Outer faces (2) $1\frac{1}{8}'' \times 2\frac{1}{2}'' \times 7''$
B Central lamination (1) $\frac{1}{16}''$-$\frac{3}{32}'' \times 2\frac{1}{2}'' \times 7''$
C Side-of-center $\frac{1}{16}''$-$\frac{3}{16}'' \times 2\frac{1}{2}'' \times 7''$
   laminations (2)

HARDWARE AND EXTRAS

D Quartz clock-watch, $1\frac{5}{16}''$ diameter—best if it has
   a push-fit rubber band friction fitting

1 Having glued and laminated the block, set the compass radius to $1\frac{1}{4}''$ and strike off the arc that makes the top of the case. Make sure that you spike the compass point on the middle of the fine black laminate.

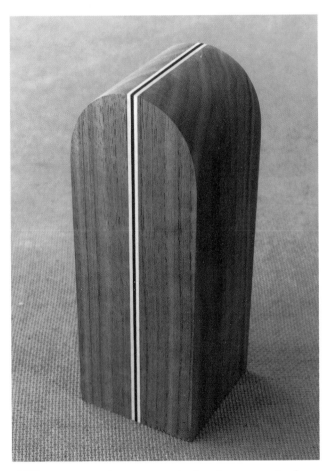

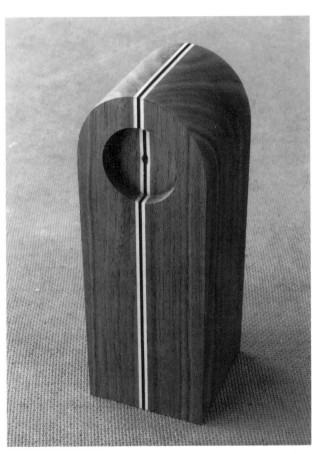

3 Having selected a Forstner bit sized to fit the diameter of your clock, sink a recess to the appropriate depth. The success of the project hinges on the hole being perfectly placed, so spend time getting it right.

2 Having cut the curve on the band saw, run the faces of the block down on a series of lapping boards. Work through the grit sizes, from a medium-fine through a super-fine flour grade. Only work in the direction of the grain, and be careful that you don't blur the sharp corners.

Swivel-Head Duck Decoy

Duck decoys are no more than carved and whittled imitations of the real thing. The word *decoy* comes from the Dutch words *kooj* and *koye* meaning to lure or entice. Though old accounts suggest that decoys were first used by Native Americans, the notion was soon taken up by the white American settlers. It's a wonderfully simple idea: The carved wooden ducks are anchored out in the water, along comes a flock of ducks attracted by the decoys, they circle with a view to settling down on the water, and—Bang!—the hunter is provided with easy targets. Okay, so it's not very sporting, but when one must. . . .

Though once upon a time duck decoys were swiftly carved and whittled by the hunters to their own design and then thrown in a corner for next season, they are now considered to be extremely valuable and very collectible examples of American folk art.

MAKING THE DUCK

Having first studied the working drawings, and variously looked at pictures of ducks, collected magazine clippings, made sketches and drawings, and maybe even used a lump of Plasticine to make a model, take your two carefully selected blocks of wood and draw out the profiles as seen in side view. Make sure that the grain runs from head to tail through both the head and the body.

When you are happy with the imagery, use the tools of your choice to clear the waste. I used a band saw, but you can just as well use a bow saw, a straight saw and a

PROJECT SIX: WORKING DRAWING

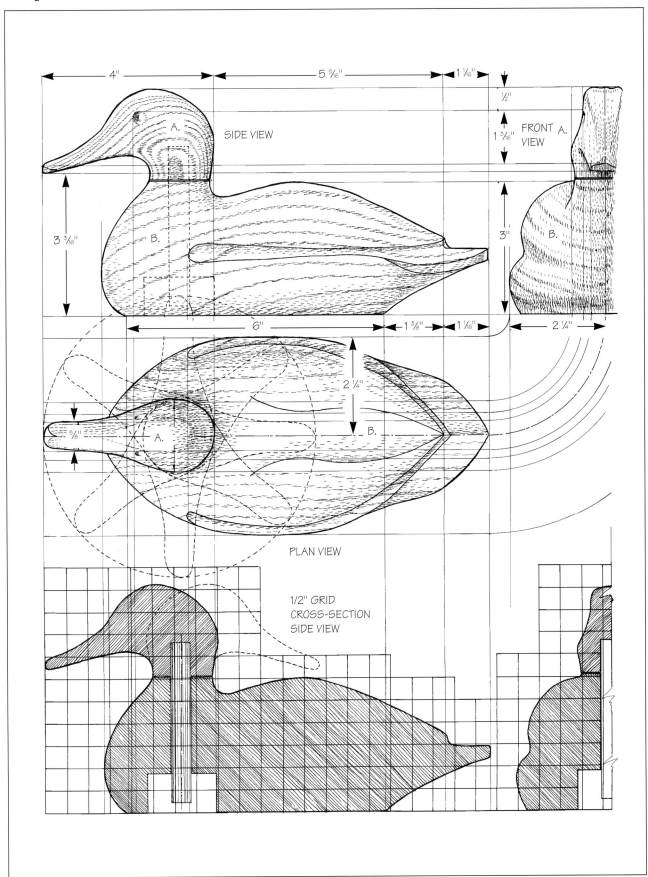

4"
5 ⁵⁄₁₆"
1 ¹⁄₁₆"

½"
1 ³⁄₁₆"

SIDE VIEW
FRONT A. VIEW

A.
B.
B.

3 ³⁄₁₆"
3"

6"
1 ³⁄₈"
1 ¹⁄₁₆"
2 ¼"

2 ¼"

⁵⁄₈"
A.
B.

PLAN VIEW

1/2" GRID
CROSS-SECTION
SIDE VIEW

rasp, a large coping saw, a gouge and a drawknife, or whatever gets the job done. Next, set the two parts down on the bench—so that you can see them in plain view—and draw the top views out on the partially worked surfaces. Don't fuss around with the details, just go for the big broad shapes. Once again, when you are pleased with the imagery, use the tools of your choice to clear the waste.

When the shapes have been roughed out, then comes the fun of whittling and modeling the details. Having noticed that this is the point in the project when most raw beginners lose their cool and start to panic, I should point out that there are no hard-and-fast rules. If you want to stand up or sit down, or work out on the porch, or work in the kitchen, or whatever, then that's fine. That said, your wits and your knives need to be sharp, you do have to avoid cutting directly into end grain, and you do have to work with small controlled paring cuts.

Of course, much depends upon the wood and your strength, but I find that I tend to work either with a small thumb-braced paring cut—in much the same way as when peeling an apple—or with a thumb-pushing cut

that is managed by holding and pivoting the knife in one hand, while at the same time pushing against the back of the blade with the other hand. Either way, you do have to refrain from making slashing strokes.

When you come to the final modeling, start by sitting down and having a good long look at the duck. Compare it to the working drawings and any photographs that you have collected along the way. If necessary, rework selected areas until it feels right. When you reckon that the form is as good as it's going to get, use a rasp and a pack of graded sandpapers to rub the whole work down to a smooth finish. Avoid overworking any one spot; it is better to keep the rasp/sandpaper and the wood moving, all the while aiming to work on the whole form.

Finally, fit the neck dowel, run a hole down through the duck, drill out the washer recess on the underside of the base and the fixing hole on the front of the breast. Block in the imagery with watercolor paint, give the whole works a rubdown with the graded sandpapers, lay on a coat of beeswax or maybe a coat of varnish, and the duck is ready . . . not for shooting, but for showing!

STEP-BY-STEP STAGES

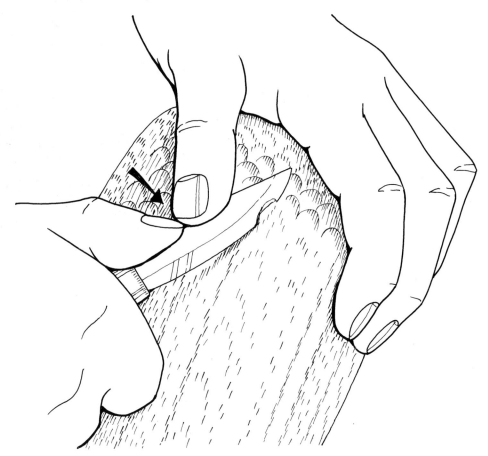

1 If you are looking to make a strong but controlled cut, you cannot do better than go for the thumb-pushing paring approach. In action, the cut is managed by holding and pivoting the knife in one hand, while at the same time pushing against the back of the knife with the thumb of the other hand. Notice how the direction of cuts runs at a slicing angle to the run of the grain.

MATERIALS LIST—PROJECT SIX

A Head (1)   1¾″×2½″×4½″
B Body (1)   3½″×5½″×10″
C Neck pivot (1)   ½″ dowel×4″ long

HARDWARE AND EXTRAS

D Glass/plastic eyes (2)

E Plastic washers to fit the dowel (2)

F Watercolor paint as used by artists: gold-yellow, red-brown, dark green, white, gray, blue and black

Note that all measurements allow for a small amount of cutting waste.

3 Use the graded abrasive papers to achieve a smooth finish. In this instance the paper is wrapped around a dowel that nicely fits the long scooped shape.

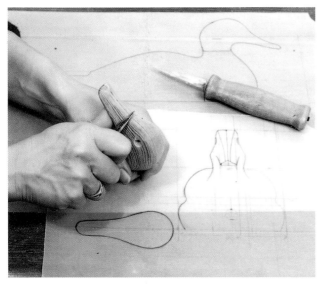

2 Use the thumb-braced paring cut to shape the characteristic duck bill. This cut uses the thumb as a lever to increase the efficiency of the stroke. Always be ready to change knives to suit the cut—a small penknife blade for details, and a large sloyd knife when you want to move a lot of wood.

4 Slide the dowel into the neck socket and adjust the fit so that the head profile runs smoothly into the body. Be mindful that you might well need to modify the head and/or the body so that the two parts come together for a close-mating fit.

5 Now, with the washer in place, ease the pin/peg through the breast hole and push it into the dowel hole. Use plastic or leather washers to ensure a good tight-turning fit.

SPECIAL TIP: SAFETY WITH A KNIFE

The degree of safety when using a knife will depend to a great extent on your stance and concentration. Okay, so there is no denying that a knife is potentially a very dangerous tool, and it's not a tool to use when you are tired or stressed, but that said, if the knife is sharp and the wood easy to cut, then you shouldn't have problems.

If you have doubts, then have a tryout on a piece of scrap wood. And don't forget . . . a good sharp knife is much safer that a blunt one that needs to be worried and bullied into action.

Matching Letter Opener and Desk Set

When I was a school kid, I was obsessed with collecting knives and boxes. I had a box with a secret compartment, a box with a swivel-and-twist lid, and best of all, I had a beautiful old pen case dated about 1880, given to me by my grandfather. As for knives, I had all manner of dirks and daggers. My favorite was a stiletto-type knife that had a silver handle and a red leather case—really beautiful! Well, you know what kids are like, I was forever making up games and adventures that involved hiding things. Anyway, to cut a long, sad story short, I

hid my special knife and box in my grandfather's garden, my vacation came to an end, and I went to school. And no doubt you have guessed when I came back a year later, everything had changed—no grandfather, no garden, no box, no knife. My grandfather had died, and my grandmother had sold the house.

This project draws its inspiration from my long-gone knife and box. The silver knife has become a carved letter opener, the box has become a pen case, and they both go together to make the perfect desk set.

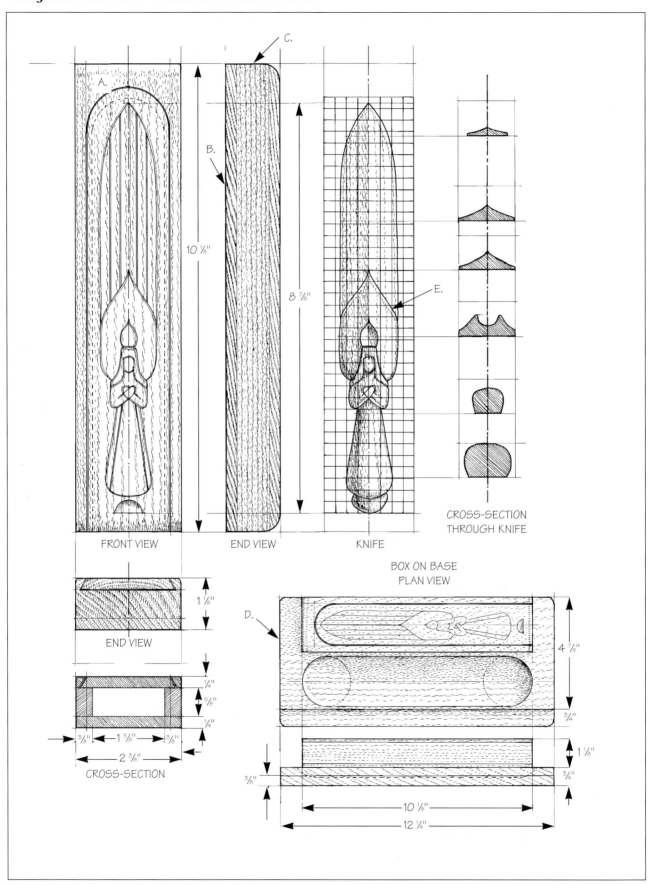

FRONT VIEW

END VIEW

KNIFE

CROSS-SECTION
THROUGH KNIFE

END VIEW

CROSS-SECTION

BOX ON BASE
PLAN VIEW

10 ⅛"

8 ⅞"

1 ⅛"

¼"

⅝"

¼"

⅜" 1 ⅝" ⅜"

2 ⅜"

4 ⅞"

¾"

1 ⅛"

¾"

⅜"

10 ⅛"

12 ¼"

A.

B.

C.

D.

E.

MAKING THE BOX

Having studied the working drawings and seen how the box is laminated up from three layers, take your three pieces of carefully chosen wood and pencil label them "lid," "middle" and "base." Set the middle section out with a center line, and use the 1⅝"-diameter Forstner drill bit and the scroll saw to clear the waste. Clean out the cavity and take it to a good finish.

Take the lid piece and use a pencil, ruler and compass to draw out the design—meaning the shape of the sliding lid. This done, move to the scroll saw, set the table to "tilt," and fret out the lid. You should finish up with a lid edge miter that undercuts the lip of the frame.

When the four component parts for the project—the base, the hollowed-out middle section, the top frame and the lid—are all nicely finished, smear glue on the mating faces, sandwich them together and clamp up. Be sure to wipe up any glue that oozes into the inside of the box, or between the top of the middle section and the undercut lip of the frame.

Finally, the box is glue mounted on a simple pen tray base. Then the whole works is cleaned up with the plane and rubbed down to a smooth, round-cornered finish.

STEP-BY-STEP STAGES

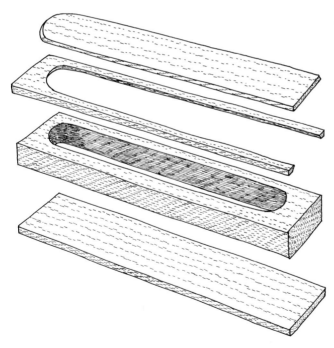

1 When you have made the four component parts for the box—the base, the hollowed-out middle section, the lid, and the frame into which the lid slides—take the finest graded sandpaper and rub the mating faces down to a good finish. Pay particular attention to the inside of the hollow and the mitered edge of the lid frame.

CARVING THE BOX AND THE KNIFE

Carefully draw out the angel design, make a tracing, and then pencil-press transfer the imagery through to both the top of the sliding lid of the box, and the piece of wood that you have chosen for the knife. This done, take the tools of your choice and swiftly set in the lines of the lid design with a V-section trench. I prefer to use the knife to cut the incised lines, but you might well prefer to use a small V-tool.

When you work with the paper knife, start by fretting out the profile on the scroll saw. This done, take a small low-angled shoulder plane and clear the bulk of the waste from the blade. When you are happy with the basic form, use a knife to whittle the details. All you do is set the primary lines in with stop-cuts and then shave the wood down to the level of the cuts, so that selected areas are left standing in relief. For example: When you come to the skirt, slice a stop-cut around the line of the waist, and then shave the wood from the hem through to the waist, until the skirt takes on the characteristic conical and rounded shape. And so you continue, working here and there over the design, all the while setting in stop-cuts and cutting in towards the stop-cuts until you achieve what you consider to be a good form.

Finally, rub all the surfaces down to a smooth finish, give the whole works a thin coat of Danish oil, and then use beeswax to burnish to a sheen finish.

MATERIALS LIST—PROJECT SEVEN

BOX

A	Lid (1)	⅜″×2½″×12″
B	Box center (1)	⅜″×2½″×12″
C	Middle section (1)	¾″×2½″×12″
D	Base (1)	¾″×5⅝″×12¼″
E	Knife (1)	¾″×1½″×9½″

Note—I used American cherry throughout.

SPECIAL TIP: CARVING THE DETAILS

If you have any doubts at all as to how the carving ought to go—meaning the shape and the modeling of the details—the best way is to make a full-size Plasticine working model. All you do is roll out the Plasticine to the required ¾″ thickness, cut out the profile as seen in the plan view, and then whittle and model the form in much the same way as you would with the wood. Making and using a model is a winner on many counts. You can easily replace the Plasticine if you make a mistake, you can use the Plasticine to make trial cuts and, best of all, you can use dividers to take step-off measurements directly from the model through to the wood.

2 Transfer the angel design through to the top of the lid, and to the knife. Be mindful that in both instances it's important that the design be perfectly aligned with the center line. Use a hard pencil so that the lines are firmly indented.

3 Use a small penknife to cut the incised lines that make up the design of the lid. Work each **V** section incision or trench with three cuts—first a single stop-cut down the center of the **V** to establish the depth, followed by an angled cut to each side of the stop-cut to remove the waste.

5 Use the three-stroke whittling method to block out and partially model the various basic forms. The working order is:
■ Define the perimeter of the form—the skirt, head or whatever—by making stop-cuts straight down into the wood.
■ Make angled cuts down into the stop-cuts to define the length and breadth of the form.
■ Use restrained easing and paring cuts to rough out the details as seen in the plan side and end views.

4 Having made a Plasticine model to help figure out the intricacies of the design, take a small nosing shoulder-type plane and swiftly reduce the bulk of the waste. Shape the blade by angling down each side of the center line.

6 The broad modeling is best achieved by using a small-bladed pen-knife to make thumb-braced paring cuts. The technique wins on at least two counts—the thumb increases the efficiency of the stroke, while at the same time giving you maximum control. The cone shape of the skirt is achieved by first running a stop-cut around the waist, and then paring down at an angle toward the stop-cut.

7 The **V** section that goes around the top of the head is achieved by repeatedly making a sequence of three cuts—a deep straight-down stop-cut to establish the depth of the **V**, followed by two cuts that angle down and in towards the bottom of the stop-cut.

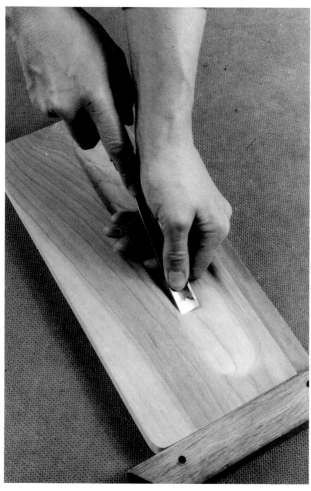

8 Once you have drawn out the shape and position of the pen tray, use a shallow sweep gouge to carve out a smooth-sided dip or depression.

USING THE SCROLL SAW

If you are new to woodworking and maybe a bit nervous, and you plan to make small fancy items like boxes, push-along toys, chair backs or pieces of marquetry—meaning items using thin sections of wood that have a lot of delicately curved fretworked profiles and pierced holes—then you can't do better than getting an electric scroll saw.

This machine, sometimes called an electric fretsaw or an electric jigsaw, is just about as safe as you can get. In truth, it is so safe that it is one of the few woodworking machines allowed in schools for young kids. In fact, I first saw one of these machines being used in a school by a ten-year-old—to make a jigsaw puzzle. Okay, so they can nip and worry fingers, but the working action is such that anything more than a grazed finger is almost impossible.

The scroll saw has a reciprocating blade, meaning a blade that joggles up and down as if to imitate the movement of a hand fret or coping saw. The bottom end of the blade is clamped in a chuck that is driven by the crankshaft, while the top end of the blade is clamped to the end of a spring-loaded arm. The blade is fitted with the teeth pointing downward, so that it cuts on the downstroke. In use, the workpiece is advanced across the worktable toward the joggling blade, and maneuvered so that the moving blade is always presented with the line of the next cut. The wonderful thing about these saws is that the resultant cut edge is so clean that it hardly needs sanding.

If you are thinking about buying and using an electric scroll saw, the following tips and pointers will help you on your way.

Saw Table—There are about six machines currently on the market—German, British, Canadian and American. Though they are all pretty good, it is most important that you get an up-to-date machine that has a table-tilt option. This feature allows you to tilt the worktable so you can make a cut that is variously angled to the working face, as in this project. A good tip is to rub over the work surface with a white candle before use. It lowers the wood-to-table friction so that the workpiece glides rather than staggers.

Blade Clamp—From one machine to another, there are all manner of weird and wonderful mechanisms used to clamp the blade. For example, one machine has a clamping block that is tightened by means of an Allen wrench/

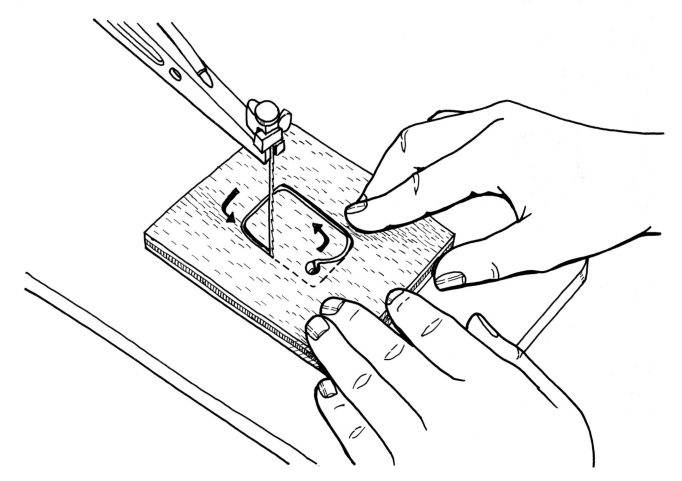

CUTTING A PIERCED WINDOW
In use, the workpiece is maneuvered and advanced so that the moving blade is presented with the line of the next cut.

key, another has a pronged finger that supports pin-end blades, and yet another has a clamping block that is tightened by means of a large thumbscrew/wing nut. While each system has its good and bad points, I think overall the large thumb-screw is the best option. I say this because the Allen wrench option soon distorts, and the pin-holding mechanism on some machines is made of butter-soft, easy-to-bend metal.

Blades—The standard scroll saw blade is 5″ long and flat-ended. Coming in a whole range of tooth sizes, from coarse through super fine, the blades are designed variously to cut everything from solid wood, plywood and plastic, to thin mild steel, brass and aluminum. If you find that the blade bends and drifts or burns the wood, then chances are it is badly tensioned and/or blunt and needs replacing.

Dust-Blowing Mechanism—When the saw is in use, the sawdust piles up and covers the line of cut so that you can't see where you are going. Though most scroll saws have a bellows and tube mechanism that blows the dust away from the drawn line, the pity of it is that the dust is blown directly into the user's face—all good fun! If this is a worry to you, then it's best to wear a face mask.

CUTTING AN INTERIOR PIERCED "WINDOW"

A good part of the pleasure of using a scroll saw is its ability to cut a perfect hole or "window" in the middle of a piece of sheet wood. For example, it is perfect for fretting out models, and for making pierced chair back slats—anything that is relatively small and intricate.

The working procedure for piercing enclosed "windows" is:

■ Drill a pilot hole through the area of waste big enough to take the blade.

■ With the machine unplugged, ease off the tension until the blade goes slack.

■ Unhitch the top end of the blade from its clamping block.

■ Pass the end of the blade up through the pilot hole and rehitch it to the top block.

■ Retension the blade until it "pings" when plucked.

■ Hold the workpiece firmly down on the table so that the blade is clear of the sides of the pilot hole, and then switch on the power.

■ Fret out the "window" until the waste falls free.

■ Finally, switch off the power and then release the tension, unhitch the top end of the blade, and remove the workpiece.

Classic Bow Saw

The classic bow saw, sometimes known as a Turner's saw, is a tool whose design and origins go way back into the dim and distant past. Though I've seen bow saws of this type illustrated on Greek vases, in English medieval manuscripts, in Albrecht Dürer's etchings, and so on, the classic design is such that it is still as useful for curved work as it ever was. The actual workings of the saw are fascinating: The blade is held under tension by means of a wooden stick or tongue and a twisted twine that is wrapped around the top of the side cheeks.

What else to say, except that if you are looking to make a unique gift for a woodworking buddy—something really special—then this is a beauty!

MAKING THE SAW

First things first—buy your blade. I say this because, if your blade is a different size than the one used in this project, you can modify the other material sizes to suit.

The bow saw is made in three parts. There are the handles that need to be turned on the lathe; the fancy frame sides or cheeks that are fretted out with a scroll saw, coping saw or even a bow saw; and finally, there are the metal parts that make up the handles. Okay, so it does sound a bit complicated, but don't panic, it's as simple as can be.

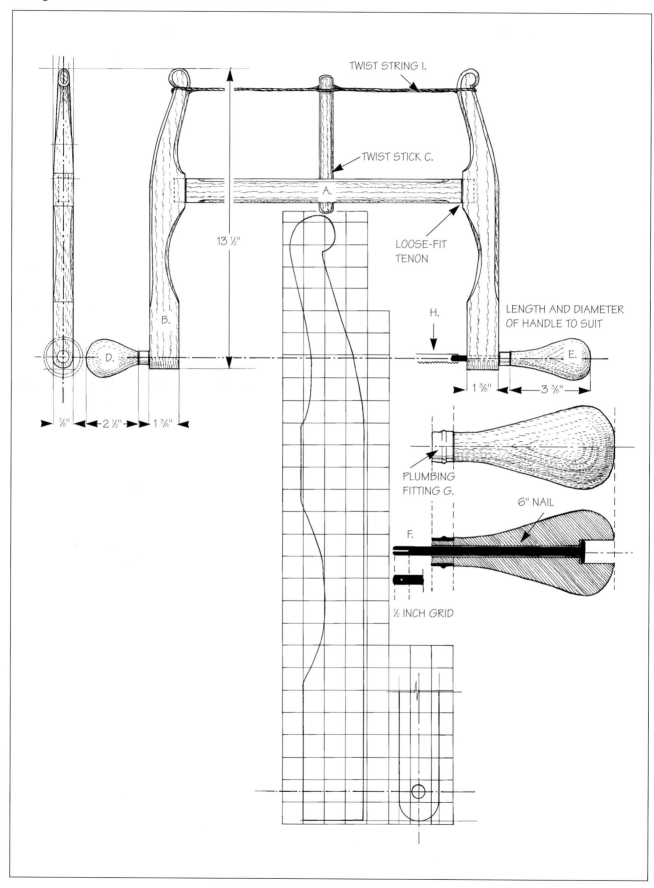

TWIST STRING I.

TWIST STICK C.

A.

LOOSE-FIT
TENON

13 ½"

B.

H.

LENGTH AND DIAMETER
OF HANDLE TO SUIT

D.

E.

1 ⅜"

3 ⅜"

⅞"   2 ½"   1 ⅜"

PLUMBING
FITTING G.

6" NAIL

F.

½ INCH GRID

SHAPING THE FRAME

Having pencil-press transferred the designs through to the wood, fretted out the shaped ends, and used a straight saw to cut out the crossbar, use a small spokeshave and a plane to skim the three component parts down to a good finish. Cut chamfered edges on the crossbar and the cheeks and generally round over the curved shapes, all as shown in the working drawings.

When you come to cutting the mortise and tenon joints—meaning where the crossbar fits into the end cheeks—all you have to remember is that the joints both need to be a loose fit. The best procedure is to cut the joint for a good push fit, and then trim the ends of the tenon to a rounded finish so that they are an easy rocking fit in the mortise.

Establish the handle centers on the bottom ends of the cheeks. Then run them through with a hole that is a loose fit for your 6″ nails. Finally, use a piece of offcut to make the twist stick, sometimes called a toggle or a tongue.

TURNING THE HANDLES

Having studied the working drawings and seen how the two handles are quite different in length, take your chosen piece of wood—we used maple—and turn the two handles in one piece. Make sure the stubs or spigots fit your metal ferrules, and then rub them down on the lathe and part off.

As to how you drill the holes through the handles, it really depends on your workshop and equipment. I found that the best way was to grip and support the handle in the four-jaw chuck—meaning the chuck on the lathe—and then use a drill chuck mounted on the tailstock end of the lathe. The good thing about this method is that it is a foolproof way of making sure that the holes are perfectly centered. All I did was drill the larger diameter recess hole and then follow through with a smaller diameter hole.

When you have made the handles, all nicely smooth and drilled, then comes the tricky business of fitting the metal parts. It's best to start by fitting the ferrules. Take your metal tube (I used two copper plumbing fittings, but you can just as well use a slice off the end of a brass tube) and cut it off so that you have two ½″ lengths or rings. Use a file and steel wool to polish the rings to a smooth, shiny finish, and then tap them in place on the turned handle stubs.

Finally, pass the 6″ nails through the handles and the ends of the frame, cut them to length with a hacksaw, and cut slots into the ends of the nails so that they fit your chosen bow saw blades. Mark the position of the blade-end holes. Then run ³⁄₃₂″-diameter holes through the nail ends, so that you can secure the blade ends with small nails or split pins.

PUTTING IT TOGETHER

When you have made all six component parts—the two scrolled cheeks, the crossbar, the two handles and the twist stick—then comes the fun of putting the saw together. Start by fitting the **H**-frame together. This done, pass the slotted nail ends through the bottom ends of the cheeks and fit the blade with the pins. Make sure that the teeth are looking away from the largest of the two handles. Wrap three or four turns of strong twine/cord around the fancy ends of the cheeks and knot the ends of the cords together to make a loop. Finally, slide the twist stick in place between the turns of twine and twist it over and over so that the cheeks pull apart and the blade is held under tension.

SPECIAL TIP

Since the bow saw cheeks are put under a lot of tension and stress, it's vital that you choose the best possible wood. I've checked around and seen that the handles are usually made from beech, maple or ebony, and the **H**-frame made from beech or ash. We have gone for an ash frame and maple handles.

MATERIALS LIST—PROJECT EIGHT

FRAME

A	Crossbar (1)	½″ × ⅞″ × 12″
B	Frame cheeks (2)	⅞″ × 2″ × 14″
C	Twist stick (1)	¼″ × ⅝″ × 6½″

TURNED HANDLES

D	Large handle	2″ × 2″ × 14″—this length allows for a good amount of turning waste
E	Small support handle (1)	

HARDWARE AND EXTRAS

F	Metal rods to hold the blade	6″ nails (2)
G	Metal ferrules	½″-diameter tube (2)
H	Bow saw blade	12″ blade twist cord, 60″ long
I	Strong waxed twine	8′ long
J	Split pin	

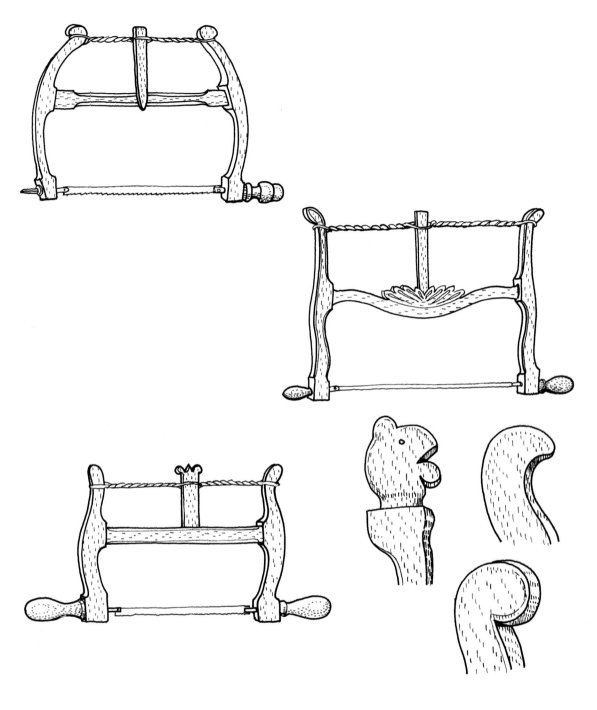

STEP-BY-STEP STAGES

1 An old English bow saw with curved cheeks and stop-chamfered details is shown at top left; an old English bow saw with unusual carved detail at top right. An English bow saw with a whittled twist stick is shown at center left; a selection of carved cheek scroll designs at center right. Shown at bottom, a European bow saw tends to be bigger, with straight cheeks and a much wider blade.

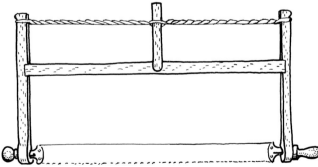

2 The three parts that go to make the **H** frame: the two scrolled cheeks and the crossbar. If you look closely at this photograph and compare it to the finished project, you will notice that I had to shorten the crossbar to fit the only available blade.

3 Trim and adjust the tenon so that it is a loose rocking fit in the mortise. Notice how the corners of the mortise need to be nipped off at an angle.

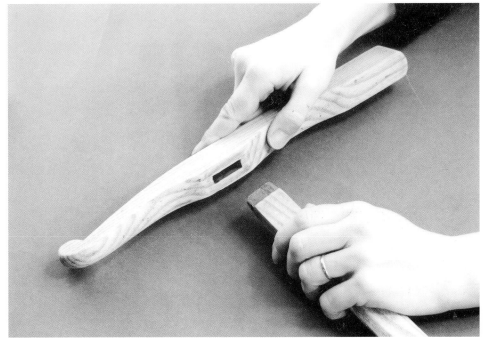

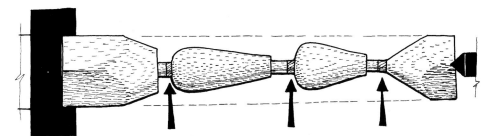

4 The on-lathe sequence—from left to right—the headstock waste, the parting waste, the large handle, the ferrule stub, the parting waste, the small handle, the ferrule stub, and finally the parting and tailstock waste. Note that the arrows indicate the parting waste.

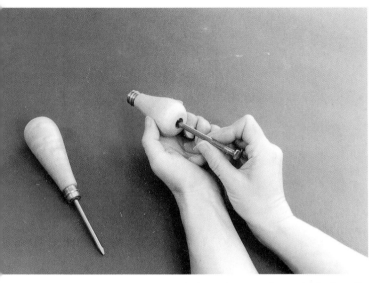

5 Bend the nail slightly and pass it through the handle for a tight captured fit. See how the nail head fits snug and flush in the recess.

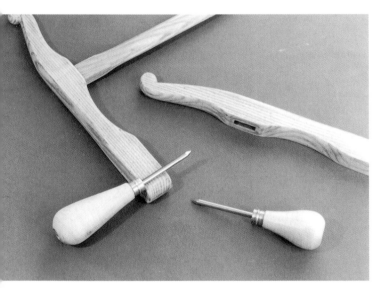

6 Check the length of the nail against the width of the frame and then mark the position of the blade slot accordingly. If you need a longer nail stub, then deepen the recess hole.

7 Slide the blade in the slot and fix it in place with a split pin. If at some time you need to fit a slightly longer blade, then you can slide washers on the nail between the ferrule and the cheek.

Carved Fruit Bowl

There is something magical about carving bowls. Do you know what I mean? One moment you have a slab of wood—nothing very special, just a piece of wood that might or might not end up on the fire—and the next moment you have a carved bowl that is a useful part and parcel of your life. We have this bowl that my Welsh grandfather made. It wouldn't win prizes and it isn't so beautiful, and it is a bit stained and has somehow been slightly scorched on one side, but for all that, it has always been with me. When I was a kid with chicken pox, the bowl was filled with apples and placed beside the bed; it was beside me when I was studying for my exams; it was given to me when I got married, and no doubt I will give it to one of my sons somewhere along the line. It has become an heirloom, something precious!

So there you go, if you are looking to make a special gift, one that might well see the next millennium in and out, then perhaps this is the project for you.

CARVING THE BOWL

Before you do anything else, you need to search out a block of easy-to-carve wood about 4″ thick, 12″ wide, and 12″ along the run of the grain. You could use a wood like lime, a fruit wood, a piece of yellow pine, or whatever, as long as it's relatively easy to carve and free from splits and knots.

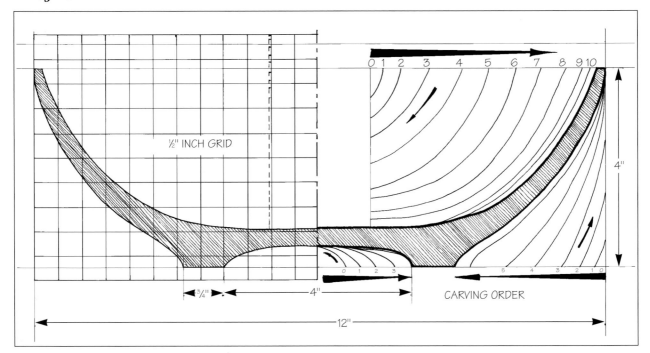

½" INCH GRID

CARVING ORDER

¾" 4" 12"

4"

0 1 2 3 4 5 6 7 8 9 10

Pencil label the two 12"×12" faces, one "top rim" and the other "foot rim." Now, with the slab set "top rim" face uppermost, first draw crossed diagonals to establish top-center; then use the compass or dividers to scribe out two circles, one with a radius of 6" and one with a radius of 5½". Rerun this procedure on the "foot rim" side of the slab, only this time have the two circles at 2¾" radius and 2" radius. When you're happy with the way the wood has been set out, use a band saw to cut out the blank. This done, move to the drill press and run a good size pilot hole into the center of the "top rim" side of the wood. Drill down to a depth of exactly 3¼". I used a 2"-diameter Forstner bit, but a 1"-diameter would be fine. Being mindful that the bottom of the hole marks both the level of the inside bowl and the thickness of the base, it is vital that you don't go deeper than 3¼".

With the workpiece set down on the bench so that the "top rim" face is uppermost, take a mallet and a straight, shallow sweep gouge and work around the rim of the drilled hole cutting back the waste. The working procedure should go something like this: Work once around the hole scooping out a ring of waste, work around this initial ring scooping out another ring of waste, and so on, all the while backing up until you reach what will become the inside rim of the bowl. When you have cleared one level of waste, return to the edge of the drilled hole and

start over. So you continue, clearing the waste level by level until you begin to establish the beautiful shape of the inside of the bowl.

Use whatever tools best do the job. For example, I started with the straight gouge and the mallet, then changed to a front-bent gouge, and finally I switched to using a small hooked knife for tidying up.

When the shape of the inside of the bowl is well established, turn the workpiece over so that the base is uppermost, and set to work carving and shaping in much the same way as already described. The carving procedure for the outside of the bowl is pretty straightforward, only this time you need to work in two directions—from the inside edge of the foot ring and in toward the center of the base, and from the outside edge of the foot ring and out and down towards the rim.

And so you resume, carving the inside of the foot ring a little, carving the bold convex shape of the outside of bowl profile, carving the inside of the bowl a tad more, and so on and on, until the wall thickness ranges between about ⅜" at the rim to ⅝" outside the foot ring. And of course, all along the way, you have to keep your tools razor sharp so that each and every cut is clean, crisp and controlled. As you get nearer to the beautiful bowl shape that is hidden just below the surface of the wood, you have to be more and more cautious with your cuts.

SPECIAL TIPS AND RULES OF THUMB

It's all straightforward, as long as you stay with the following guidelines:

■ Try to set up a work rhythm—carve for a few minutes, then stroke the tool on the stone and strop, then stand back and be critical, and then go back to a few minutes of carving, and so on. You will find that this way of working ensures that everything is controlled . . . the tools stay sharp, you have time to assess your progress, and you don't get tired.

■ As the bowl nears completion, you will find that it is more difficult to grip and hold the bowl. The best way is to either cradle it in your lap or nestle it on a pile of rags.

■ When you are carving the inside of the bowl—when it's nearly finished—you have to be extra careful that you don't lever on and break the relatively fragile rim. To prevent this end, you might need to use one of the bent gouges rather than a straight gouge. I would recommend either a no. 5 bent gouge at about ¾″ wide, or perhaps a no. 7 spoon gouge at about the same width. Be mindful that the flatter the sweep (meaning the shape of the blade in cross section) the greater the chance that the corners of the blade will cut and tear the wood.

STEP-BY-STEP STAGES

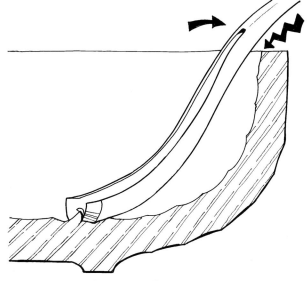

CARVING THE BOWL INTERIOR
The swooping shape of the bent gouge lets you carve the concave curve without levering the shaft of the tool on the fragile rim.

MATERIALS LIST—PROJECT NINE

A	Piece of wood (1)	4″×12″×12″—with the grain running along the length, meaning across the bowl

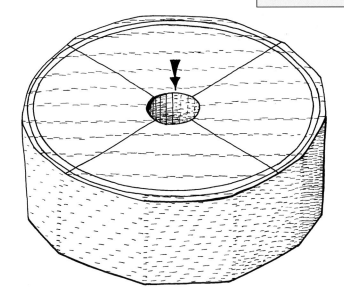

1 Having established the center of the square slab by drawing crossed diagonals and cutting the circular blank, use the 2″ diameter Forstner bit to run a 3¼″-deep pilot hole down into the center (top). Work around the hole clearing the waste (bottom left). Clear the waste level by level, all the while backing up from the pilot hole through to the rim (bottom right).

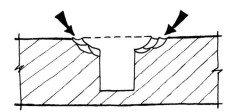 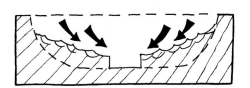

2 One of the easiest ways to bring the bowl to a good finish is to use a hooked sloyd knife. As you are working around the inside of the bowl, be mindful that all along the way you will need to adjust your angle of cut to suit the ever-changing run of the grain.

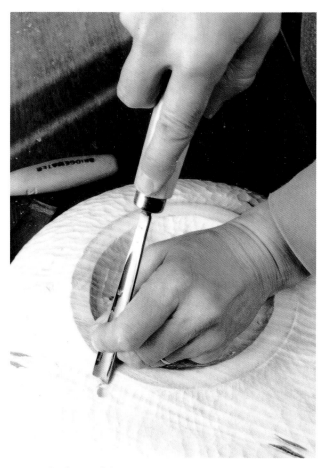

3 When you come to carve the inside of the foot—meaning the inside of the base ring—use small, controlled cuts, with one hand pushing and the other guiding and being ready to break. Notice how in this instance you can lever the shank of the tool on the relatively strong foot rim.

4 The beautiful concave curve shape that runs down from the outside of the foot rim is achieved by thrusting down with the blade and levering back with the handle.

5 All along the way you will have to make repeated checks with the caliper. Try to aim for a section that starts relatively thick at the base and gradually tapers up to a thin rim.

A GOOD WOOD GUIDE FOR CARVING

Woodcarving is a wonderfully fulfilling and exciting area of woodworking, but only, if you choose the right wood. When I first started carving, I had in mind to carve a female torso, a Venus. I'm sure you know what I mean, a bit like Marilyn Monroe, but more so. Though my teacher told me to use lime, when I arrived at the wood yard and saw the astronomical prices, I was swiftly talked into buying—at a quarter of the price of lime—a massive piece of I-don't-know-what.

Well, when I got my "bargain" wood back to the workshop, it was a nightmare. The wood was green and wet, it was full of iron-hard knots, it started to warp and split the moment I started carving, it made my tools rusty, the grain was wild and twisted—I could continue listing its terrible qualities. Yes, I did manage to finish my carving, but at what cost to my strength and sanity? It was truly awful, a sort of mad mix-up between Marilyn Monroe and a glandular Guernsey!

The moral of this sad little tale from my teenage years is there are no shortcuts, and there are very few bargains. You *must* use a piece of good wood. The following listing will help you on your way:

Alder—A sapwood tree common in low-lying areas. A wood traditionally used by North American Indians and early settlers, it is especially good for bowls and general kitchenwares.

American Whitewood—Known variously as tulipwood, basswood, canary wood, and many other names besides, this is a soft, easy-to-carve wood.

Apple—A hard dense, close-grained fruitwood, it comes in small sizes, carves well and takes a good polish. Apple is traditionally used for small items of treen (woodenware), and for kitchenwares.

Beech—A heavy, relatively easy-to-carve wood that has a yellow-gold sapwood and a reddish heart. Beech is particularly good for carved furniture.

Boxwood—A beautiful, pleasant-smelling, butter-smooth wood that is extremely hard and close-grained. If you want to carve items like jewelry, hair combs, small dishes and boxes, then boxwood is a good choice.

Cedar—Pencil Cedar is a favorite wood for carving. It cuts to a clear pink-brown finish.

Cherry—American cherry is a close-grained, hard-to-work, reddish brown wood that comes in relatively small widths. It carves well and can be brought to a wonderful high-shine finish.

Hickory—Straight-grained with a white sapwood and reddish brown heartwood, hickory is often the first choice for large sculptural carvings.

Horse Chestnut—White if it is felled in winter, and yellow-brown if it is felled later in the year, this wood is especially good for carved furniture details and for dairy and kitchenwares.

Holly—A close-grained, ivory-white wood that carves well and takes fine details, it is a good wood for small desktop toys, and kitchenwares.

Lime—English lime is one of my favorite woods. Butter-colored, close-grained and easy to carve, it is the traditional choice for architectural work, like mirror surrounds, coats-of-arms, small sculptures and interior trim. Though linden or basswood are often described as being the same as lime, they are to my way of thinking quite different.

Maple—Soft maple is the traditional choice for general carvers—used for making such things as furniture, domestic wares and musical instruments—while rock maple is preferred for heavier items like sports gear and some laundry wares.

Pear—A pink-brown wood that has a close-grained, satiny finish. It's really good for kitchenwares.

Plum—One of my favorite woods. Though it is certainly very difficult to carve, the color and texture are special—especially good for small presentation pieces.

Sycamore—A hard, light-colored wood, it carves and finishes well. Sycamore is a top choice for dairy and kitchenwares, where it is important that the wood leave no smell or taint.

Yellow Pine—White to reddish light brown, it is good for large sculptural carvings and interior details. It has been used traditionally in shipbuilding and interior joinery. If you order the wood unseen, be sure to specify "smooth first growth." If you don't, there is a good chance that you will be given poor-grade, coarse and knotty second growth.

Gilded Scroll Shelf

My dictionary defines a console shelf as being an ornamental bracket—especially one used to support a bust—while a scroll is described as being a decorative carving in the form of a stylized roll of parchment. Okay, not very exciting·you might think, just a shelf and a bracket. But give the shelf a semicircular form and an ogee-type lip profile, embellish the scroll with a wee bit of carving and coat of gold paint, and then put the two together, and suddenly—Pow!—you have a really special eye-catching item, a truly unique and dynamic piece of woodwork.

MAKING THE SHELF

The actual shelf is very straightforward—really no more than two half-circles butted and dowelled at right angles. That said, you do have to be mindful at the layout stage that the top board—the one that will become the shelf surface—needs to measure the radius of the circle from front to back, plus the thickness of the wood.

Use a compass, ruler and square to set out the wood: Fret the two forms out with a band saw. Use a router or moulding plane to cut the lip profile. Then use glue and hidden dowels to butt the forms together at right angles.

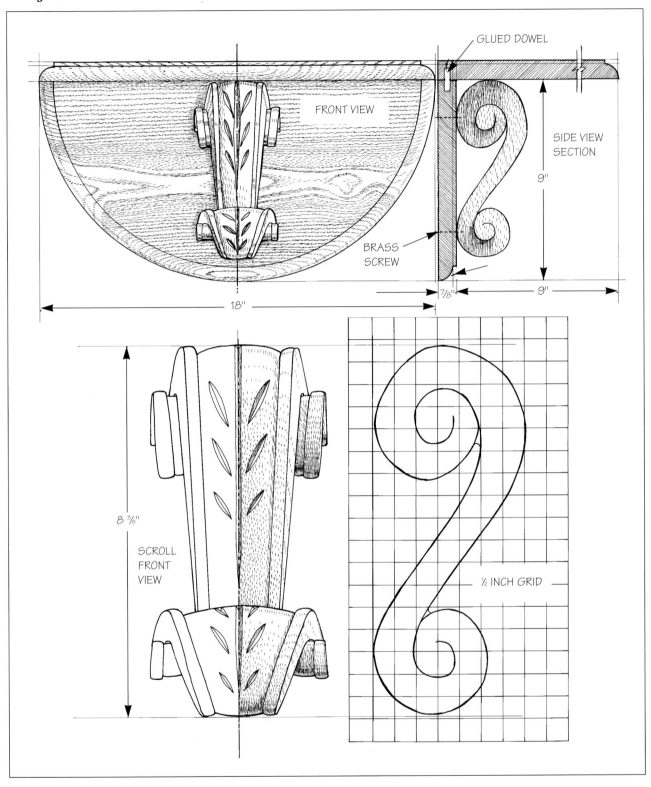

FRONT VIEW

GLUED DOWEL

SIDE VIEW
SECTION

9"

BRASS
SCREW

18"

7/8"

9"

8 3/8"

SCROLL
FRONT
VIEW

½ INCH GRID

MAKING THE BRACKET

Having chosen your block of easy-to-carve wood, press transfer the side view of the scroll through to the wood and then cut it out on the band saw. Then run a center line down the front face. Next, take some masking tape and use it to establish the tapered shape of the scroll as seen in front view.

Set the workpiece side-down on the bench and use a mallet and shallow-sweep straight gouge to lower the side of the scroll. The best way of visualizing the lowered side of the scroll is to think of it as a mountain road that starts at the center of the big end of the scroll, curls around and downhill, and then slowly back uphill to finish at the center of the small scroll. Staying with this mountain-and-roads imagery, if you leave the scroll on its side, and if you lower your viewpoint to bench level, you will see that with the finished scroll, the scroll centers—or you might say the peaks around which the roads curl—are both at the same height. When you are clear in your own mind as to the shape of the scroll, carve down to the level of the "road" on one side of the scroll, then flip the scroll over and work the other side in identical mirror-image reverse. The best way of ensuring that the scroll is symmetrical as seen in front view is to slightly lower the "road" on one side and then the other, and then back to the other side, and so on. You will find that this little-by-little approach—with constant reference to the center line—is the easiest way to proceed.

Having made the sides of the scroll, turn it over so you can see it front-on. Use the masking tape and a soft pencil to establish the ¼"-wide track that runs parallel to each side edge. When you are happy with the guidelines, use a knife and gouge to work and model the central area until it is lowered by about ³⁄₁₆" and is slightly convex.

When you have what you consider is a well-formed and modeled scroll, use the graded sandpapers to rub it down to a smooth finish. Make sure that all the nooks and creases are crisp and clean. This done, draw the stylized foliage imagery on the front face of the scroll, incise it with the knife, and then give the whole works a coat of matte white undercoat paint, followed by a coat of best-quality gold paint.

Run a couple holes in from the back of the shelf support, use brass screws to fix the bracket to the shelf, and finally give the whole works a coat of thin varnish and/or a burnishing with beeswax polish.

SPECIAL TIP

Though generally in woodcarving your wood has to be attractive, straight-grained, free from splits and knots and relatively easy to carve, there are times when, as the wood is to be painted, you don't have to worry about its looks. This being the case, you could go for an inexpensive, characterless but easy-to-carve variety like jelutong. That said, if you relish the notion of the project but want to go for a uniform plain wood blond look, then I think your best choice would be lime.

STEP-BY-STEP STAGES

1 Butt the two halves of the shelf together and fit with glue and secret dowels.

MATERIALS LIST—PROJECT TEN		
SHELF BRACKET		
A Top of shelf (1)	⅞"×9⅞"×18"	
B Back board (1)	⅞"×9"×18"	
C Carved bracket (1)	4"×5"×10"	
HARDWARE AND EXTRAS		
D 2" brass countersunk screws (2)		
E White matte undercoat paint		
F Best-quality yellow-gold paint or gilding paste		

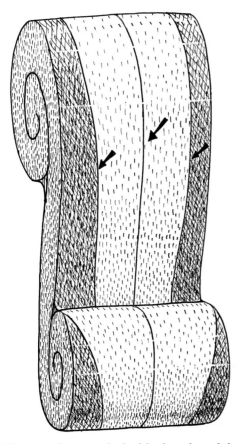

2 When you have made the blank and used the masking tape to establish the shape of the bracket as seen in front view, shade in the waste that needs to be cut away. Note that the arrows indicate the center line and the sides.

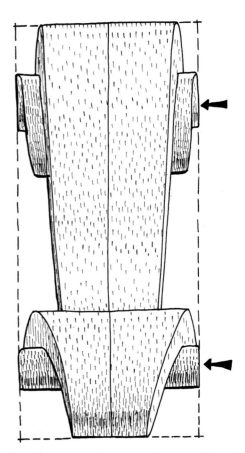

3 If you have carved it correctly, you will see that the scroll peaks are at the same level.

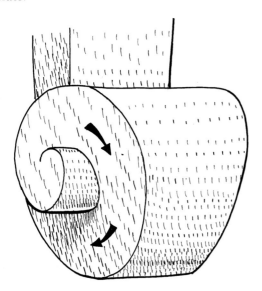

4 The mountain road analogy perfectly describes how the side-face curls down, around and up. Be watchful as you lower the "road" that the "cliff" face—meaning the face that in this view goes vertically up from the road and through to the peak—is cleanly worked.

5 Use a knife to clean up the sides and to deepen the stop-cut that defines the depth and shape of the camber.

7 Be careful when you are working the top of the small scroll that you don't dig too deeply into what will be end grain.

6 The incised cuts are best worked with three strokes: one stop-cut to set in the center line and to establish the depth of the incision, followed up by an angled cut at each side to establish the width of the incision and to remove the waste.

8 Having used a ruler and square to draw in the center line, do a dry-run fit of the scroll. Establish the position of the screw holes by taking your eye-level down to the face of the wood and identifying the scroll-to-shelf contact points.

GILDING THE SCROLL BRACKET

Woodworkers are forever coming up with new and exciting ideas. I'm sure you know what I mean. One moment you are half way through a project, and the next . . . Eureka! A new idea or variation springs to mind. And so it was with this project. The moment I had finished describing how to carve the bracket and give it a lick of gold paint, it suddenly occurred to me that perhaps it would be more in keeping with the wood carving tradition to gild the bracket.

Though gilding is a technique that requires a good deal of time and patience, the end result is stunning, well worth the effort. There are two methods of gilding: oil and water. I have opted for what is best described as the shortcut oil technique. That is to say, I follow the whole procedure for the gold painting, as already described on page 56, and then finish up with the gilding.

THE GILDING PROCEDURE

Give the finished carving a couple of coats of matte white undercoat paint followed by a coat of gold paint, and wait for the paint to dry. Then take a piece of fine-grade sandpaper and rub the carving down to a smooth-to-the-touch finish—the smoother the better.

Being mindful that the oil gold size dries in about 25 minutes, give a small area at the back of the bracket a swift thin coat. When the size is tacky—almost dry—slide one of the gold leaf sheets out onto the plywood and cut it into small postage-stamp pieces. Press straight down with the full length of the blade.

Now for the tricky part! Take the brush or tip, pass it a couple of times over your hair to increase the static, and then touch it down so that it picks up a small piece of gold leaf. Lay the gold leaf down onto the tacky size and dab it into place with a pad of lint-free cotton cloth. Take up the second piece of gold leaf and lay it down alongside the first so that there is a slight overlap. Continue until the whole surface of the bracket is covered in gold.

Finally, dust the surface with a dry brush to remove loose pieces of gold, and the job is done.

MATERIALS LIST: OPTION

A Quick-drying oil gold size

B 25-leaf book of gold leaf—or metal leaf (imitation gold) at a quarter of the price

C Gilder's brush or tip

D Craft knife blade

E Piece of easy-to-hold plywood (12″ × 12″)

STEP-BY-STEP STAGES

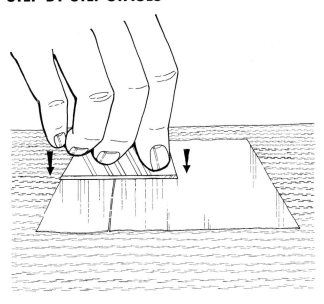

1 Having made sure that everything is clean, dry and free from dust—your hands, the blade and the plywood—take the blade and press the whole length of the cutting edge down hard on the gold leaf. Make the cut by slightly rocking the blade.

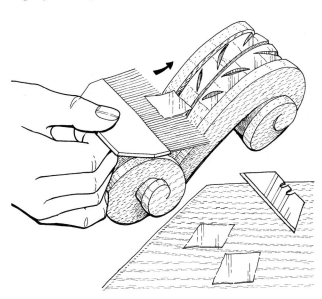

2 Wipe the brush over your hair to increase the static, then swiftly pick up the gold leaf and lay it down on the tacky gold size. Press the leaf down with a clean cotton pad.

COMBINATION AND MULTIPLANES

I don't like routers. Okay, so maybe they are the best thing since sliced bread. Yes, they do a wonderful job, and I agree that they aren't as expensive as they used to be, and there is no doubting that they get the job done in almost no time at all. I know all the arguments. The thing is, I don't like routers because of all the dust and noise. But how do I cut my moldings, grooves, tongues, rounds, hollows and all the other profiles? Well, the beautifully simple answer is, I use an old Stanley 45 combination plane.

The Stanley 45 is, to my way of thinking, one of the most beautiful woodworking tools ever invented.

It came into being at the end of the nineteenth century, when there was a huge push by the iron plane manufacturers to come up with a single do-it-all plane. You have to remember that up until that time, every type and size of slot, tongue, fillet and fancy profile needed to be worked with a dedicated plane. Can you imagine? If you were a keen woodworker in the nineteenth century, it's likely you would have needed 40 to 50 or more different wooden moulding planes!

The Stanley 45 is a quality tool, more like a hand-built gun than a plane. It has a main body piece with a sledge-skate sole runner and a rosewood handle; a cutter clamp and integral depth gauge with a large knurled wheel; two nickel steel outrigger arms that are fixed to the main body with screws; a middle section with an integral handle and sledge-skate sole runner that fits onto the outrigger arms; a fence with a rosewood runner; and a selection of 45 plus cutting irons. And as if all that isn't enough, my Stanley 45 is covered in fancy caste motifs; dripping with chrome and nickel plate; heavy with thumbscrews, locking nuts, wing nuts, adjusting screws, cutting spurs and knobs; and supplied with the set of cutting irons packaged in a wooden wallet. Better yet, the whole works fits into the most attractive tin presentation box.

And just in case you are wondering . . . yes, the plane does indeed live up to its looks. Of course, it has to be carefully tuned and the irons need to be kept sharp, but that said, it is a most efficient tool.

Setting up the Plane

As to why Stanley stopped making the "45" way back in the 1960s, who can say. They are still being sought by today's woodworkers, and though they are relatively easy to obtain, the main problem is that most secondhand 45's come disassembled and without the necessary setting, tuning and using instructions.

And just in case you are one of the growing army of avid user-collectors who have a secondhand Stanley 45, and would dearly like to know how it needs to be sorted

STANLEY COMBINATION PLANE
The legendary Stanley 45 in action.

and tuned, then help is at hand.

The order of setting up or tuning—the way I do it—is as follows. I first select a cutting iron and check that the edge is clean and well honed. If necessary, I wipe it on the oilstone and use a slipstone and a strop to bring the cutter bevel to a razor-sharp, 35° edge. This done, I fit the cutting iron into the groove and adjust the wing nut so that the iron is held in position. Next, I slide the middle sole runner on the outrigger arms and slide it up to the body of the plane so that the blade has a runner at each side edge. If I am going to cut across the run of the grain, I set the spurs so that the little cutter or nicker blade is in the down position. Lastly, I measure and set the fence and the plane is ready for action.

Okay, the plane is well set up and tuned, you have a nice straight-grained piece of wood in the vise, and you are ready to go. The first thing to do is get a household candle and wipe it over the sole and fence of the plane. Certainly it sounds a bit strange, but a couple strokes with the candle will dramatically reduce the friction—it will just about cut your sweat by half. And just in case you don't believe me, try it without the candle—ha!

When you are ready to go, with the depth gauge set, set the runners down on the workpiece so that the fence is hanging over the side edge of the workpiece. Clench that fence hard up against the side edge, and then take repeated passes until the groove, tongue or profile is cut. The best procedure is to start at the end of the wood furthest away from you, and then gradually back up. Of course, you might need to adjust the depth of cut, but if you have it all together, with the plane nicely tuned and set up, the rest is easy.

As I said at the beginning, the Stanley 45 is a beautiful tool: no dust, no deafening noise, no need for a mask or ear plugs, no motors or dangling cables. Just a sweet slickkk . . . slickkk . . . as the paper-thin shavings curl up.

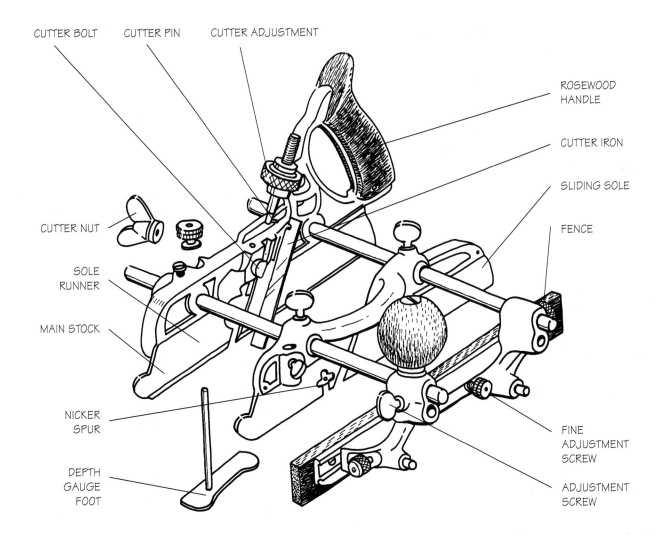

CUTTER BOLT   CUTTER PIN   CUTTER ADJUSTMENT

ROSEWOOD
HANDLE

CUTTER IRON

SLIDING SOLE

CUTTER NUT

FENCE

SOLE
RUNNER

MAIN STOCK

NICKER
SPUR

DEPTH
GAUGE
FOOT

FINE
ADJUSTMENT
SCREW

ADJUSTMENT
SCREW

STANLEY PLANE ANATOMY

Heart-Shaped Puzzle Box

When I was a kid, an old woman left me a small wooden box in her will. The funny thing was that, although it appeared to be just an ordinary empty box with a small division to one side, when I shook it, it rattled. After variously pushing, pressing and sliding the sides and base of the box, I discovered that it had a secret compartment! It was very exciting. When I pressed down on one side of the bottom inside of the box, I was able to slide up one side of the little division to reveal a secret space. As for the rattling noise, it was a solid gold half sovereign!

This project draws its inspiration from that old wooden box. It has all the same elements: a secret area, a sliding lid, and a part that swivels open.

MAKING THE BOX

First things first, you must have a good long look at the working drawings and see how the box works. Of course, like all such boxes, it's pretty easy when you know how. To open the box, swivel the lid to the right to reveal the coin slot and the top of the dovetail key. Then, at the same time, slide and swivel the coin slot face of the box down and around to reveal the inside compartment.

When you have studied the design, draw out the heart shape. Make a tracing. Pencil press transfer the traced lines through to the layers of wood that go to make up the box. You need six layers in all: four at ¼″ thick and two at 1⅛″. Fret the shapes out on the scroll saw, so that they are all slightly oversize—meaning that the line of cut

PROJECT ELEVEN: WORKING DRAWING

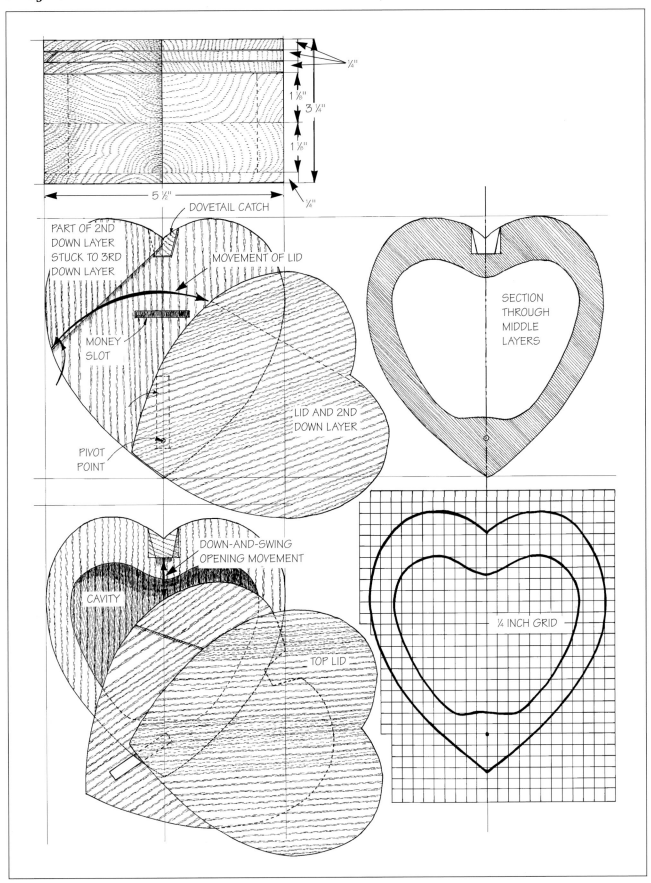

¼"

1⅛"

3¼"

1⅛"

¼"

5½"

¼"

DOVETAIL CATCH

PART OF 2ND
DOWN LAYER
STUCK TO 3RD
DOWN LAYER

MOVEMENT OF LID

SECTION
THROUGH
MIDDLE
LAYERS

MONEY
SLOT

LID AND 2ND
DOWN LAYER

PIVOT
POINT

DOWN-AND-SWING
OPENING MOVEMENT

CAVITY

TOP LID

¼ INCH GRID

is about ⅛″ to the waste side of the drawn line. While you are at it, cut out the inside-box area.

Glue the two 1⅛″ layers together and use a gouge to pare the inside of the box to a clean finish. Next, use a fine saw and chisel to pare a channel from top to bottom of the box (at top-middle, where the two cheeks meet). Now, pencil label the four ¼″-thick cutouts: "top," "second down," "third down" and "bottom." Then glue the "bottom" to the box.

Glue the rod of wood in the channel and cut the dovetail shape. This done, take the "third down" layer and cut the two slots and the dovetail location notch. When you are happy with the fit, take the "second down" layer, set the scroll saw cutting table at an angle, and run the wood through the saw to cut the miter across the top-left cheek.

When you have made all the component parts, then comes the not-so-easy part of putting the box together. The best procedure is to first fix the slotted layer and the bottom half of the mitered layer with a swivel screw. Then glue the two halves of the mitered layer together. Finish by gluing the top layer to cover up the swivel screw.

Certainly it sounds complicated but, in fact, you will have it worked out in much less time than it takes to tell. Finally, you rub it down with the graded sandpapers and seal with Danish oil.

SPECIAL TIP

The secret of getting this box right has to do with the standard of the finishing and fitting. All the surfaces must be rubbed down to a super-smooth finish, especially the mating faces that are to be glued and the faces that are to slide over each other. As to the final gluing, the best procedure is to start off using double-sided sticky tape, and then use the glue for real when you know how it all goes together. I say this because it is the easiest thing in the world to make a complete mess-up by gluing the wrong two parts together. Be warned!

MATERIALS LIST—PROJECT ELEVEN

A Board (6)	¼″×6″×7″—I used English yew throughout

HARDWARE AND EXTRAS

Swivel screw (1)	1¼″-long brass countersunk screw

STEP-BY-STEP STAGES

1 Detail showing how the square rod fits in the channel so that the dovetail at the top locates in the slotted layer. The procedure is to first glue and fit the rod, then cut the dovetail.

2 The miter cut on the second layer needs to be angled so that it looks toward the bottom of the heart. Be mindful that the finer the saw used to make the cut, the better the fit.

3 See how the top-left part of the mitered layer needs to be glued to the slotted layer, so that the topmost part of the miter hangs clear of the dovetail.

4 The pivot slot on the third layer needs to be adjusted so that the layer can be slid down and then swung over—so that the "cheeks" at the top of the heart just clear the dovetail.

5 In my design, the slotted layer is able to swing to the left or right. If you want to make the box more of a puzzle, a good modification would be to build in a little "stop" peg so that the layer could only be swung to the left.

TWEAKING THE DESIGN

When you are fixing the swivel point and the slot, make sure that the slot is long enough for the cheeks to clear the underside of the dovetail.

6 Because I had quite a lot of trouble cutting out the center of the box—first with the drills and then with a gouge—I think the next time around I will redesign the dovetail post so that it cuts right through the wall of the box. Then I can more easily clear the inside-box waste on my fine-bladed band saw.

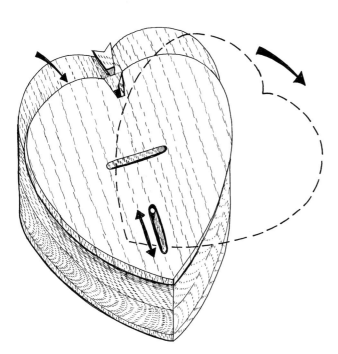

PROTOTYPES

A prototype is a full-size working model that is made prior to the project. The idea is to use inexpensive materials to work out all the problems before you start using your precious materials.

As you can imagine, this heart-shaped box didn't drop from the sky perfect and ready-made—no way! In fact, it was rather difficult to sort out. Although the various views and cross sections looked fine on paper, I just couldn't figure out how the three layers that make the top of the box fit great together. In the end, after a deal of swearing and messing about, I decided that the best way was to make a full-size prototype from three pieces of ¼″-thick hardboard.

The working procedure went as follows: First I cut out the three heart shapes and pencil labelled them "1," "2" and "3." Then I drew the heart shape out on the bench. Next, I took cutout number 3 and played around on the drawn-out heart with various placings of the swivel point and the sliding slot.

The main difficulty I found was positioning the miter in such a way that there was enough room for the "cheeks" of the heart to slide open.

When I had established the precise position of the swivel point and the length of the slot, I then tried out board number 2 and fixed the position of the miter slot. And, of course, when it came to making the box for real, I had the hardboard cutouts to use as templates.

And just in case you are thinking that you are so skilled that you can go straight in and make the toy, the table or whatever, without making a working model, yes, you might well be lucky once or even twice. But sooner or later you are going to make a mistake with one or all parts getting incorrectly cut and/or glued.

For example: I once designed the most beautiful chair. It looked wonderful on paper; the drawn elevations were a work of art! But when it was built, it was unstable, it was grossly uncomfortable, and it started to pull apart. Another time, I made a moving toy that looked good on paper, but when I made it full size, the friction between the wheels and the floor was so great that it simply didn't work.

All this is to say that the only sure way of knowing that a design is going to work is to make a full-size working model.

Traditional Springerle Board

The American Colonial kitchen or "keeping room" was an absolute treasury of fine woodwork. There were butter bowls and salt trays, boxes and knife racks, pipe-shelves, cutting boards, tables and chairs, all of them variously carved, pierced and detailed. Of course, they are all exciting in some way or other, but for my money, I particularly like the beautifully carved biscuit and cookie boards. There were shortcake molds made by the English and Scottish communities, breadboards made by the Swedish communities, little stamps and presses made by the Polish immigrants. Just about every Old World group had a unique style, form and tradition of carved boards.

Of all these "mother country" woodenwares, the German American Springerle cookie boards are perhaps the most delicate and fanciful. Every early Pennsylvania German home had them. The cookie dough was rolled thin and the carved hardwood board was pressed onto it to imprint the designs. When the cookies were baked, the resultant raised designs and motifs made an attractive table arrangement.

So if you like the notion of basic carving, and you know someone who enjoys baking, then this could be the project for you.

PROJECT TWELVE: WORKING DRAWING

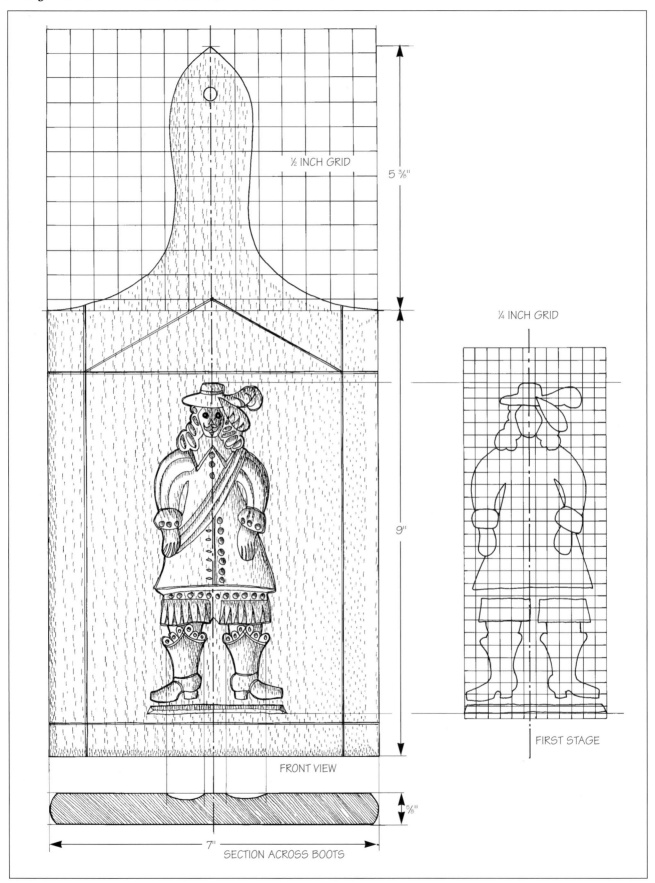

½ INCH GRID

5 ⅜"

¼ INCH GRID

9"

FIRST STAGE

FRONT VIEW

⅝"

7"

SECTION ACROSS BOOTS

MAKING THE SPRINGERLE BOARD

This is the perfect project for nervous beginners who are looking for an easy way into the craft of woodcarving. All you need is a flat board, a bench clamp or holdfast, a V-section gouge, a straight gouge, a small spoon gouge, a sharp knife and a steel safety ruler, and you are ready to begin.

Trace the design on a slab of well-prepared, close-grained hardwood. We have chosen beech, but you could just as well go for plum, pear, sycamore or maple. Then carefully pencil-press transfer the primary lines of the design through to the wood. Next, cut out the shape of the board on a scroll saw and rub the edges down to a good finish. This done, secure the workpiece flat-down with the clamps or holdfast and use the spoon bit tool to scoop out the primary elements of the design. Don't try for any great depth, just settle for nice round depressions. It's all pretty easy, as long as you are careful that the tool doesn't dig too deeply into the grain and/or skid across the wood.

Continue working with a controlled action, holding and guiding the tool with one hand and pushing, scooping and maneuvering with the other until you have achieved what you consider is a good strong design. You need to dish out the hat, the hair, the face, the coat and cuffs, and the boots. Being mindful that the design is in reverse, try to judge the depth of the carving so that the fullest part of the design has the deepest hollows. Aim to scoop out the little dips and hollows to a depth of about ¼″. Don't dig the tool too deep or try to lever the tool, but rather work with a delicate scooping and paring action. Cut across the grain wherever possible. Remove only small curls of wood and try to keep the carving crisp and controlled. If you feel at any time that the tool is cutting roughly, then approach the grain from another angle or sharpen the tool with a few strokes on the stone and leather. Bear in mind that each and every hollow needs to be worked smoothly—no rough surfaces or undercuts. It's a good idea from time to time to test out your carving by taking a piece of Plasticine and pressing it into the cut shapes, just as if you were pressing dough on the board. Once you have considered the shape and detail of the pressing, you can adjust your work accordingly. Ask yourself as you are working, could the little dips be deeper? are the shapes nicely rounded? and so on.

With the basic pattern in place, take the very smallest spoon gouge and scoop out the little dips that go to make up the small dot and dash details of the buttons and eyes.

Next, use your knives to cut in the fine details. For example, you need to cut in the features, the sash and belt, the tassels around the top of the boots, and so on. And of course, if at any time along the way you want to cut in pockets or bigger plumes or other details, then follow your fancies. Finally, use the knife or V-tool to cut in the simple frame shape.

STEP-BY-STEP STAGES

1 Go over the transferred lines with a soft pencil and then spray with pencil fixative to prevent smudging.

MATERIALS LIST—PROJECT TWELVE	
A Board (1)	⅝″ × 7″ × 15″—a piece of prepared wood like beech is best

Note that all measurements allow for a small amount of cutting waste.

2 Use one of your spoon bent gouges to scoop out all the little hollows and depressions that will make up the design.

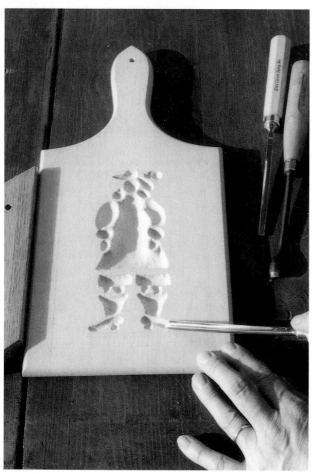

3 If the shape of the depression permits, cease with the spoon bit and change to using the straight gouge. You will find that the straight tool allows you to get a bit more weight behind the thrust.

4 Use the smallest spoon bit gouge to "winkle" out the small dot-and-dash details of the eyes and trim. Stab the tool down vertically and twist it on the spot so that it "drills" out a pocket of waste.

SPECIAL TIP

If you find that your tools are cutting roughly, the chances are that the wood is damp or unsuitable or the tools are blunt and need sharpening. The best way to work is to set yourself a rhythm. That is, spend a few minutes carving and a few minutes standing back and assessing your progress, and then a few minutes rubbing the bevel of the knife or chisel on the fine stone, and so on. If you do this, the work will move along smoothly, with the carving being nicely considered and the tools kept at maximum sharpness.

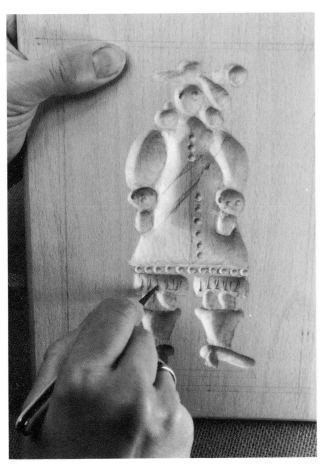 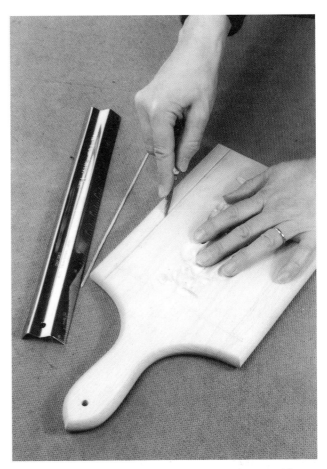

5 Use the knife to cut the tassel details. Make three cuts for each tassel—a deep stabbing horizontal stop-cut to define the width of the tassel, followed by two downstrokes to clear the waste from the triangular pocket.

6 Use the steel safety ruler and the knife to cut the V-section frame detail. Each line is made with three cuts—a single straight-down stop-cut to define the depth of the **V**, followed by two angled cuts to clear the waste.

CHOOSING AND USING WOODCARVING TOOLS

There are so many woodcarving tools on the market that beginners are often bewildered when it comes to buying gouges and chisels. For example, I have just looked through a handful of current catalogs and I see hundreds of slightly different tools to choose from. Maybe you aren't going to need more than a handful of tools, but the big problem is which ones to buy.

The first question you have to ask yourself is what do you have in mind to carve? Are you excited about the notion of carving huge sculptural pieces? Or do you fancy carving intricate little birds? Or do you just want to try your hand at traditional flatwork like chip or relief carving, the sort of carving that you see on furniture?

When you decide on your area of woodcarving—sculptural, relief designs, miniatures or whatever—it's best to buy a modest starter kit of, say, four tools. For example, you might get a couple of straight gouges, a V-tool and a bent gouge. Of course, once you actually start carving, the whole problem sorts itself out. You will soon discover that certain tricky details simply cannot be worked, or that you can't carve an undercut or some other detail with any one of your four tools. Then you have enough knowledge to buy a tool of a shape and size to suit. When I first started carving, my favorite tool was a medium-size, shallow-curve straight gouge—it still gets used more than any other tool. So you might start out with the four tools, and everything will be fine and dandy, until the time comes when you need to use a fishtail or a smaller spoon gouge, or yet another size straight gouge . . . and so the fun begins.

All that said, the single thing that bothers most beginners is that they are confused when it comes to the names and the numbers of woodcarving tools. If you don't know what I mean, look at various woodcarving tool catalogs.

From one manufacturer to another, there are all manner of descriptions that relate to the same tool types. Some manufacturers use letters and numbers, some use their own prefix codes, and so forth.

If you are a beginner and still undecided as to the correct gouges for your starter kit, then try the following method—it may help. Start by determining the width of blade you need. Let's say that you have chosen a ½″ width. Next, consider the hollow or sweep of the blade. Ask yourself, do you want a shallow sweep or do you want a deep U-section sweep for bowls and such? Finally, decide on the profile or shape of the blade along its length. For example, do you want a straight blade or a curved or spoon bent? Once you have sorted out the blade width, the shape of the sweep and the profile of the blade, then all you do is walk into the store and point a finger.

STRAIGHT CHISELS AND GOUGES

If you are still confused as to terms, the following glossary will show you the way.

Straight Chisel—A straight chisel is a flat-bladed tool that has a straight cutting edge. If you jab the cutting edge into the wood, it will leave a straight cut, like a dash. The term "straight" relates to the shape of the blade along its length. The size of the chisel is determined by the width of the cutting edge. In use, the chisel is held in one hand and then either pushed or struck with a mallet.

Straight Gouge—Though the straight gouge is straight along its length—just like the straight chisel—the blade is hollow-curved in cross section. If you stab a gouge into the wood, it makes a curved cut, like a **C** or **U**. The shape of the curve is termed the "sweep." So when you are ordering a gouge, you need to know the width of the blade and the shape of the sweep. In use, the straight gouge is either pushed by hand or struck with a mallet.

CURVED OR BENT CHISELS AND GOUGES

Having established that the term "straight" describes the shape of the blade along its length, it follows that the terms "curved" or "bent" also describe the blade along its length. For example, you might have two gouges that make identical cuts, the only difference being that one is straight along its length and the other curved or bent. They make the same cut, but the bent tool allows you to

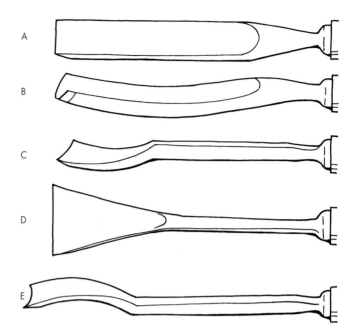

CURVED OR BENT CHISELS AND GOUGES
(A) Straight chisel; (B) deep sweep curved gouge; (C) shallow sweep spoon bent gouge; (D) shallow sweep fishtail gouge; (E) shallow sweep backbent gouge.

hook and scoop into hollows that the straight tool is unable to reach. Spoon bent, fishtail and back-bent tools are simply gouges that are more extremely shaped along their length. So, if you want the cutting edge of your gouge to be a certain width and sweep, you have to make a decision as to the shape of the blade along its length. Do you want a straight blade for heavy pushing or mallet work, a bent one for digging out a shallow bowl, a spoon shape for scooping out deep hollows, or a fishtail for cleaning out tight corners?

Handles—Once you have decided on the width of the blade, the size of the sweep—meaning the shape of the **C** section—and the shape of the blade along its length, then comes the choice of the handle. There are turned hardwood handles, plastic handles, handles with and without ferrules, and so on. I personally prefer the "London" pattern of turned and shaped octagonal boxwood handles on three counts. They are comfortable to hold, they look good, and best of all, the octagonal section prevents the tool rolling about or falling off the bench and doing damage.

Nautical Clock and Weather Station

When we decided to move from a wild and windy part of the coast to a relatively mild hills-and-dales part of the country, we felt that we wanted to take a lasting memento with us. As we both love the sea, we felt that we wanted a reminder of our wonderful walks along the rugged cliffs, of the picnics on the lonely beaches, and of the exciting times we had with our many boats. After a great deal of thought that took in such notions as collecting sea shells and the like, it suddenly came to us. Why not take a piece of driftwood—perhaps part of an old boat—and turn it into a nautical clock and weather station? To our way of thinking, the whole project would be a lasting memento . . . of the beaches, the storms that smashed up the boats, and the constant need to keep one eye on the time, tide and weather.

So if you, too, want to make a memento gift that uses a piece of found wood, then this is a great project.

The wonderful thing about a design of this size, type and character is its flexibility. There are any number of amazingly exciting options. I say this because, as soon as I had made the sculpted and weathered board, Gill came up with the beautiful idea of using one of our old moulding planes to create a classic moulded board. Her thinking was that there must be thousands of woodworkers out there who own an old plane and are just looking for an excuse to tune it up and get started! She also had the bright idea that with a more formal board, the various instruments could be arranged so that the board could be mounted vertically or horizontally.

MAKING THE FOUND WOOD BOARD

This project is slightly unusual in that your found wood needs the minimum of preparation. Okay, it needs to be clean and the like, but that's about it—no jointing, no

PROJECT THIRTEEN: WORKING DRAWING

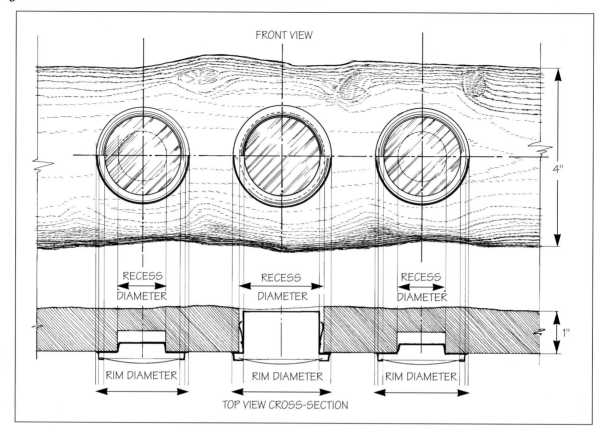

FRONT VIEW

4"

RECESS DIAMETER

RECESS DIAMETER

RECESS DIAMETER

1"

RIM DIAMETER

RIM DIAMETER

RIM DIAMETER

TOP VIEW CROSS-SECTION

extensive marking out, just three drilled holes and a small amount of planing and sanding. And, of course, there's no reason why your piece of found wood can't be a branch from a special tree, a part of an old house, a piece of wood found in the desert or mountains, or by a river, as long as it has some particular significance.

When you have found your piece of wood, set it down on the bench and consider how the instruments might best be placed. Are you going to settle for the clock, the thermometer and the hygrometer, (see page 73), or are you going to go for additional instruments like a tube barometer or maybe a special tide-time clock? Of course, much depends on the size of your piece of found wood.

Though I wanted three matching brass dials, with a clock having Arabic numerals, I found it impossible to get a good matchup. As you can see, I had to settle for a slightly nasty white-face clock with Roman numerals. Make sure that the instruments you choose are designed to fit into a shallow recess or hole, with the brass surround or rim overlapping the edge of the hole.

When you have decided where the instruments are going to be placed, use a wire brush to scour the grit and grime from the workpiece. If you see some part of the found wood that could be modified in some way, then so

much the better. For example, I knocked out two rusty old nails and wire brushed the resultant iron-stained holes so that they were big enough to take a piece of found rigging cordage, so that the clock and weather station could be hung on the wall.

Use the wire brush to sculpt the form, to extend and exaggerate the actions of nature. You can make contours that are rounded and rippled, much the same way as the wind, rain, sand and sea scour out the soft part of the grain, so that the hard grain and knots are left standing in relief.

When you have achieved what you consider is a good form, use a plane and sandpaper to prepare a level seating big enough for the instruments. Aim for a flat smooth surface that is slightly bigger than the instruments. Make sure that there are no nails, grit or other matter in the areas that are going to be drilled.

Having cleaned up the seating for the instruments so that it resembles a level plateau, bore the recess holes out with the Forstner bits. Then seal with a coat of varnish and use beeswax to burnish the whole works to a rich sheen finish. Finally, push fit the instruments in the holes, fit the rope or chain, and the project is finished and ready for hanging.

MATERIALS LIST—PROJECT THIRTEEN

A Board (1)   A piece of found wood of a
                      size and thickness to suit
                      your instruments.

STEP-BY-STEP STAGES

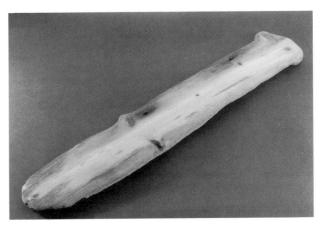

2 Remove the more obvious bits of rubbish—old nails, bits of tar, embedded grit and such. Wipe the wood with a damp cloth and leave it until it is good and dry.

1 Having found your piece of wood, select a set of instruments to fit.

3 Not forgetting to wear gloves and goggles, use a power drill fitted with a wire brush attachment to scour out the loose grain. The safest procedure is to have the workpiece either screwed or clamped to the bench.

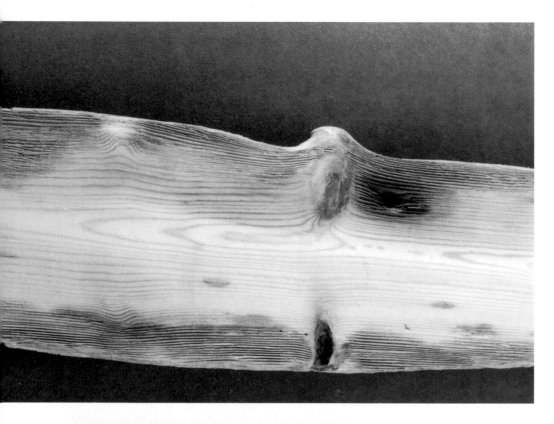

4 A close-up showing how I have concentrated use of the wire brush along the edges and around the knots, so that there is a smooth, level central area.

5 If you have a drill bit size that fits the instrument, then so much the better; otherwise, you have to drill the nearest size hole. After drilling the hole, painstakingly file it to fit. I needed to remove an all-round strip about ⅛" wide.

Note—as I said earlier in the project, I don't much like the clock as shown. On consideration, I would much prefer the little watch-clock as shown in the miniature mantle clock case project.

MAKING A TRADITIONAL BEAD-MOULDED BOARD

Having measured and marked out the board and cut it to size, use the bench plane to bring it to a smooth finish. When you are happy that the board is square and true, secure it to the bench so that one long side is hanging over the edge.

Set your moulding plane up with ⅜"-wide beading iron. If like me, you are using a single-bead cutter to plane two beads side by side—a double reed—then adjust the fence to the position for the bead that is furthest in from the edge. The procedure is: First cut the bead that is furthest in from the edge. Then reset the fence and cut the bead nearest the edge. You repeat the procedure for the other edge of the board.

Finally, having used a block plane to chamfer the ends of the board, drill out the three large-diameter holes as already described in step 5.

SPECIAL TIP

If you are looking to bore out clean-sided, flat-bottomed holes—relatively shallow holes as in this project—then you can't do better than using Forstner drill bits in conjunction with a drill press. We use a large Delta bench drill press. It doesn't wobble, or make odd noises, or require a great deal of attention. It just gets on with the job. As for the drill bits, we have a set of Forstner bits made by Freud. They do a beautiful job every single time. They bore down through end grain and hard knots, and just about anything we care to throw at them. Best of all, we like the fact that we can use them to bore out overlapping holes.

Yes, they do cost about twice as much as most bits, but they last longer, stay sharp and are a pleasure to use.

MATERIALS LIST: OPTION	
Board (1)	¾"×5¼"×15"—cherry

STEP-BY-STEP STAGES

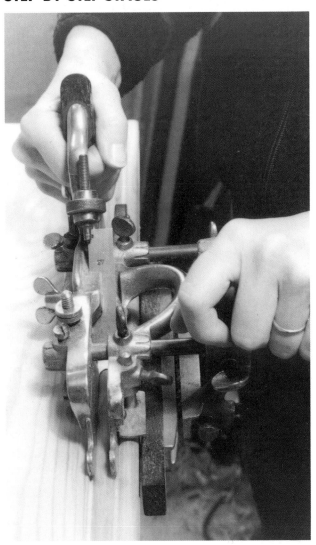

1 When you have used the plane to cut the two beads side by side, reset the blade to the very finest of skimming cuts and burnish the surface of the wood to a sheen finish. Be careful not to force the pace. Just let the weight of the plane do the work.

Raised Letter Address Plaque

When we first got married, one of the joys and pleasures was having our own home. Some of the first things we did when we moved into our infinitesimally minute cottage were to paint the front door bright red and design an address plaque. The red door didn't go down too well, but the plaque was a huge success! The neighbors admired it, the mailman said it added a touch of class—in fact the whole street made comments. So, if you want to make someone a unique gift, one that will beautify their home—be it ever so humble a house, cottage, bungalow, farm, ranch or riverboat—then a fretted address plaque is a great idea.

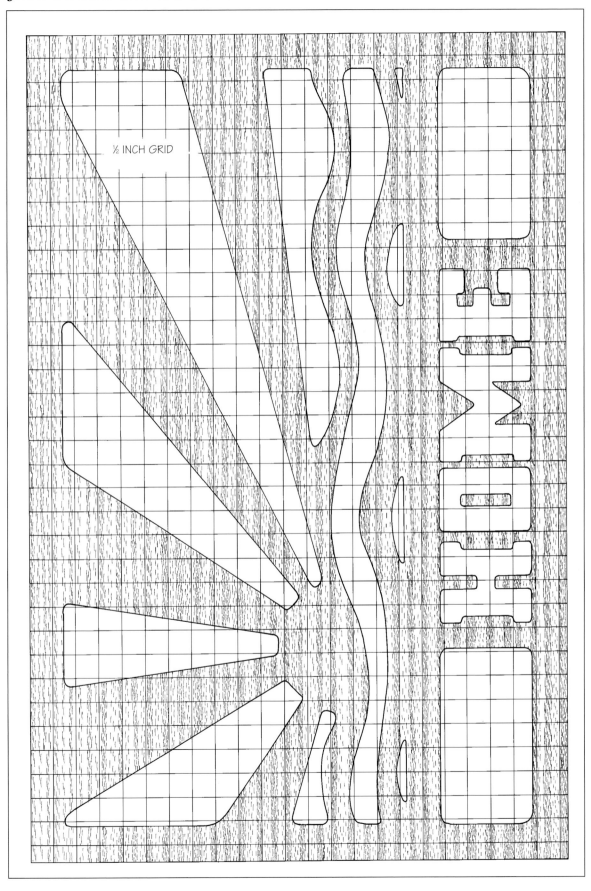

½ INCH GRID

THOUGHTS ON DESIGN

Of all the projects in the book, the name board is perhaps both the easiest and the most complex. I say this because, while the fretting techniques are truly easy—just about as simple and direct as can be—the design is something again. The problem is, of course, how to achieve a good visual effect—meaning a balance between the solid wood and the pierced areas—while at the same time getting the message across and achieving a structure that is sound. For example, it's no good at all having a design that is so complex that it needs to be viewed closeup with a magnifying glass, or a house name that is more an epic saga than one or two words. Also, the shape of the pierced areas needs to be carefully thought through so that the imagery is rounded and easy to cut. You don't want lots of spiky, sharp-angled imagery that is almost impossible to cut.

We are not suggesting that you necessarily use the sunburst image and the word "Home." After all, it would be more than a little bit strange if you, your neighbors and all our readers had identical boards. What we have in mind is that you use our imagery as an inspirational guide. In fact, you can use just about any imagery that takes your fancy—birds, horses, cattle, mountains, trees or whatever. The chief design problem is being able to link the name and the imagery so that the total message gets across. Let's say, for example, that you are giving this board to your grandmother who lives by the sea in a cottage called "Harbor View." You might well have a galleon riding the waves, or seashells, or a crab, or an anchor, or gulls, or a steamer, or whatever sea-salt-and-briny imagery that suits. And your great aunt—the one who lives in the mountains—could have a plaque with peaks, or bears, or fir trees. So let your imagination run wild!

MAKING THE PLAQUE

First things first, you need to decide on the wood. I say this because in many ways the choice of the wood is essential to the design. While the wood must withstand the wind and the rain and be relatively easy to work, it must also be fitting for the task. For example, while oak is a good choice for our plaque which is to remain unpainted and mounted on a cottage near the sea, if you live in a pine forest or you plan to have the board painted, then you might as well use an inexpensive wood like pine.

When you have chosen your wood, and once you have achieved what you consider is a good design—with the spelling of the name double-checked—trace off the design, press transfer the imagery through to the wood, and shade in the areas of waste that need to be cut away. This done, take your drill and run pilot holes through the shaded areas. How you fret out the waste areas depends on your particular tool kit. I used an electric scroll saw, but you could just as well use a coping saw, a bow saw or even a large fretsaw.

No matter your choice of tool, the procedure is much the same. Make the pilot holes. Unhitch the saw blade and enter it through the hole. Refit the blade and adjust the tension. Then variously move and maneuver both the workpiece and the saw, so as to run the line of cut to the waste side of the drawn line.

When you have fretted out the design and used the graded sandpapers to rub the rough edges to a smooth finish, cut out the base board and bring it to a good finish. Use waterproof glue to bond the two boards together.

Finally, having first protected the wood with oil, paint or whatever seems appropriate, it's time to present the board as a gift. And if you really want to make it special, you could offer to mount the board on the wall, gate, post or other appropriate place.

SPECIAL TIP

If you are going to mount the board directly on a wall, say beside the front door, it's best to use brass or bronze screws and have the board distanced from the wall by an inch or so. That way, when the rain runs down the wall and dribbles behind the board, there is space enough for a good flow of drying air.

MATERIALS LIST—PROJECT FOURTEEN	
A Front pierced board (1)	½″ × 11¾″ × 18″—we used oak
B Base board (1)	½″ to ¾″ × 11¾″ × 18″

STEP-BY-STEP STAGES

1 Having settled on a good, easy-to-work style of lettering, spend time drawing the letters up to size.

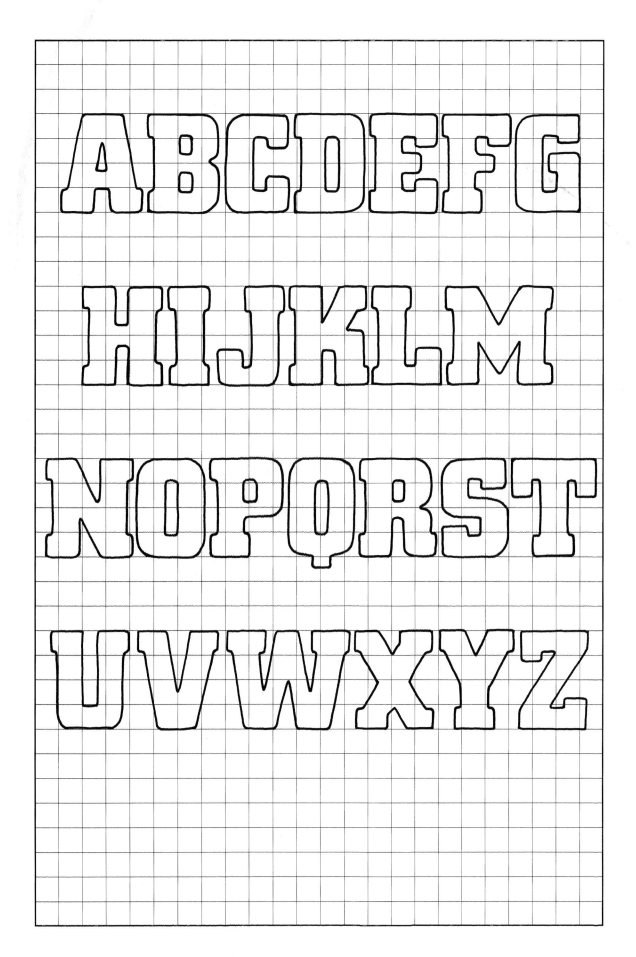

2 Run small pilot holes through the areas that need to be cut away. Be mindful if you are using a hand saw, that as some blades have pin fixings, you will have to choose a larger bit size.

3 As you can see, I had a bit of trouble keeping the line of cut on course. The problem was that the blade needed changing, the wood was amazingly tough and stringy, and I needed a rest. The only good thing you can say is that the bad cuts occur well to the waste side of the drawn line.

4 If you find that the workpiece doesn't want to move smoothly, then it's a good idea to rub a wax candle over both the surface of the cutting table and the underside of the workpiece. And don't be stingy with the blades. If the blade looks saggy or burns the wood, then change it!

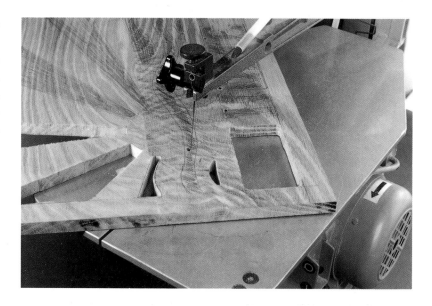

FRETTED LETTERS IN RELIEF

If your workshop is anything like mine, you are forever wondering what you can do with the offcuts. Well, there we were fretting out the letter shapes when one of the kids next door, Michelle Edwards, asked me if she could have the "M" and "E" waste cutouts from the word "HOME," so that she could stick them on her bedroom door. And so it was that the idea came to us that we could design a house board that used the cutouts rather than the holes, if you see what I mean.

PROCEDURE

First, you need to draw the letter and/or number forms up to size—ours are 1½" high—and trace them off. Arrange the tracing on the ¼" wood so that the grain runs from side to side through the letters. Pencil press transfer the traced lines through to the wood.

As for the fretting out procedure, it's much the same as already described (see page 80), only easier. If you think about it, you will see that you only have to run the pilot holes through the enclosed forms—like the **O** and **A**—and you don't have to worry about saving the ground around the letters. All you do is run the line of cut in from the edge of the wood, travel around the letter and then move on to the next form.

Once you have beveled off the edges of the ground board, then comes the tricky task of setting out the various guidelines. I use the word *tricky* advisedly, because if the spacing between the letters is wrong, or the baseline on which the letters sit is crooked, or whatever, then the whole thing will be messed-up. The best procedure is to work the spacing out on tracing paper, and then use a square and straight edge to very carefully mark the base board with all the guidelines.

When you are happy with the guidelines and the spacing, smear the back of the letters with the PVA glue and dab them down on a piece of scrap wood to remove the excess. Then position them on the board and press down firmly. With all the letters/numbers in place, stand back to check the alignment and then leave them be until the glue has set. Finally, drill the four fixing holes and give the whole works a generous coat of yacht/spar varnish.

MATERIALS LIST: OPTION

A Board (1) prepared ⅞"×4" piece of American oak at a length to suit the name of your house

B Board (1) ¼"-thick piece of American oak— enough for all your letters

C Exterior PVA glue

D Yacht varnish

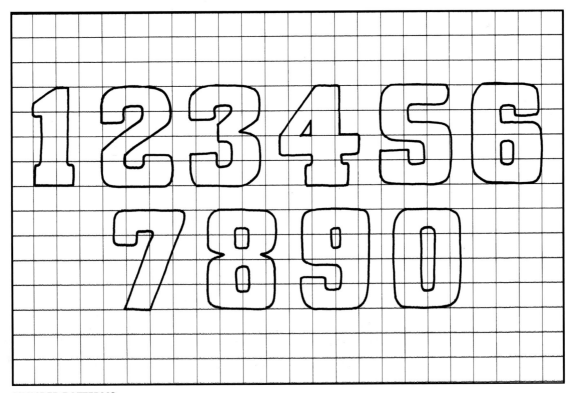

NUMBER PATTERNS

1 Press transfer the various letters and numbers through to the ¼″-thick wood. Shade in the waste so that there is no doubting the line of cut. Then fret out the letters and numbers on the scroll saw. Work at a very steady, easy pace, all the while making sure that the line of cut is fractionally to the waste side of the drawn line.

2 Check and double-check the spacing. Label the back of each letter "glue side," and then very carefully glue them in place. Do your best to avoid using so much glue that it oozes out.

DESIGNING AND TRANSFERRING

One of the chief difficulties for many woodworking beginners is that they make mistakes when it comes to designing and transferring. They make the first mistake when they draw the designs up to size, and the second when they transfer the designs through to the wood. The pity of it is that, by the very nature of things, the designing and transferring mistakes occur in the early stages. What invariably happens is that the beginners get so frustrated with the techniques of designing and transferring—what with using the wrong paper and with pencil lead getting smeared all over the paper and the wood—that they give up on the project before they ever get around to the wondrously exciting woodwork.

If you are having difficulties, then the following tips will help you sort out your problems.

Designing

Designing is the procedure of working out the structure, pattern and form of a project by making various drawings, taking photographs and making models or prototypes. For example, with this address plaque the lettering needed a lot of thought. The problem was that while I personally prefer what might be described as classic Greek and Roman letter forms—with serifs and thick and thin strokes—it was pretty plain to see that such a style would be totally unsuitable in terms of wood and fretsaw work.

So we searched around in books until we came up with a strong, bold letter style, one that looked as if it might lend itself to being fretted out with a scroll saw. Then we modified the style slightly so that all the little angles became curves. We used a ruler and square to draw the letters to size on thin layout paper, and then, using tracing paper with ruled guidelines and a square, we played around with the spacing of the letters until the word looked right. Be warned that you must always use a square in all lettering projects. If you don't, you will finish up with a badly spaced, wobbly mess!

We did much the same thing with the sunburst design. Having settled on the idea of the sunburst, we drew the elements of the design on scraps of layout paper. We fiddled around with the placing and the size and then drew up a master design on white illustration board. Then we took a final tracing.

It sounds a bit complicated, but the whole idea of working in this way is that all the many roughs, ideas, alternatives, variations, scribbles and sketches are worked out on the relatively inexpensive layout paper, before they are ever transferred to the quality paper.

We take a tracing from the master drawing so that we can use the tracing in the workshop—where it generally gets creased, damaged and used to destruction. The master drawings, however, are stored safely away for next time.

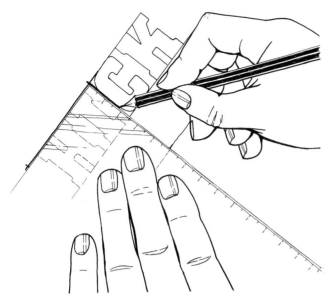

DESIGN TOOLS
A set square is an essential piece of drawing equipment. It's best to get the see-through type so you can see what's going on under the square.

Paper, Illustration Board, Layout and Tracing Paper

We use layout paper for the initial scribbles and sketches, good-quality glazed white illustration board for drawing out the master designs, and best-grade tracing paper for the transferring. It's not that we are fussy or faddish, and it's certainly not that we can afford to splash our money around. It's just that over the years we have learned that using the choice papers generally gets the job done faster and with fewer mistakes. Certainly you might think that we could use a flimsy-grade tracing paper for transferring, but again, experience has taught us that using a cheap-grade paper is a bad bet. It tears easily, it bleeds when used with ink and it doesn't take kindly to being scratched and scraped. And the same could be said about the pencils, the illustration board and all the other designing materials—the best is cheapest in the end! All that said, you can cut costs by visiting a printer and buying offcuts and ends of rolls/packs.

Masking Tape

We use an all-purpose paper, low-tack sticky tape to secure the card and tracing paper to the drawing board, and the tracing paper to the wood. We never use transparent tape simply because it is too sticky and damages both the paper and the wood.

Gridded Working Drawings

A scaled square grid can be placed over a working drawing so that the object illustrated can be reduced or enlarged simply by changing the size of the grid. For example, if the grid is described as a "1″ grid" or "one grid square to 1″" and the object is 6″ long, and you want to finish up with an item 12″ long, then all you do is double the scale and read each square off as being 2″. And, of course, when you come to drawing the design up to size, you simply draw up a grid of the suggested size and transfer the contents of each square in the design through to your drawn grid.

Tracing and Pencil-Press Transferring

I usually describe the procedure of taking a tracing from the master design and then transferring the design through to the surface of the wood as "pencil-press transferring."

The procedure is: Work up the design on layout paper, make the master drawing with a hard pencil and take a tracing with a hard pencil. Next, pencil in the back of the tracing with a soft 2B pencil. Turn the tracing right side up, fix it to the wood with tabs of masking tape, and then rework the traced lines with a hard pencil or ball-point pen. This done, remove the tracing and rework the transferred lines on the wood. Finally, spray the surface of the wood with artist's fixative to prevent the pencil from smudging.

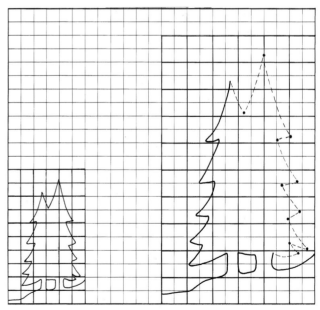

TRANSFERRING SCALED DRAWINGS
Having drawn a grid over the original design and another grid at a scale to suit—in this case I wanted to double up, so it is twice the size—then all you do is painstakingly transfer the contents of each square.

Counterbalance Horse Toy

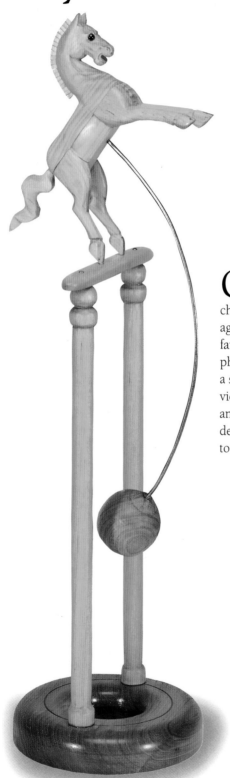

One of the pleasures of making a traditional toy of this size, type and character is the fact that you can change the specifications, the working drawings, the imagery, and the techniques to suit your own needs and fancies. For example, you might prefer to go for an elephant or a tiger rather than the horse, or you might want a straight-sided slab rather than the turned base. Our advice is to have a good long look at the working drawings and the various photographs, and then either copy our design directly or go your own way and adjust the designs to suit.

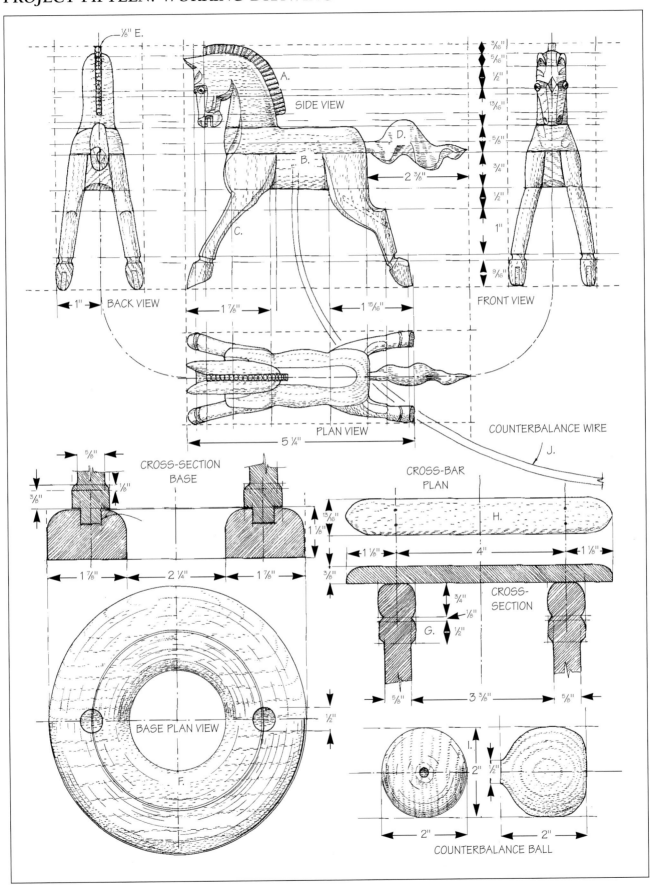

⅛" E.

SIDE VIEW

A.

D.

B.

2 ⅜"

C.

BACK VIEW

1"

1 ⅞"

1 ¹⁵⁄₁₆"

³⁄₁₆"
⁵⁄₁₆"
½"
¹³⁄₁₆"
⅝"
¾"
½"
1"
⁹⁄₁₆"

FRONT VIEW

PLAN VIEW

5 ¼"

COUNTERBALANCE WIRE

J.

CROSS-SECTION
BASE

⅝"
⅛"
³⁄₈"

1 ⅞"   2 ¼"   1 ⅞"

BASE PLAN VIEW

F.

½"

CROSS-BAR
PLAN

H.

1 ⅛"   4"   1 ⅛"

³⁄₈"

¹³⁄₁₆"
1 ⅛"

CROSS-
SECTION

¾"
⅛"
½"

G.

⅝"   3 ⅜"   ⅝"

I.

2"   ½"

2"   2"

COUNTERBALANCE BALL

MAKING THE HORSE

Having roughly fretted out the shape of the head and the four legs, begin by taking the seven component parts—the head, the four legs and the two body pieces—and gluing them together to make the blank. The best procedure is to first glue the two body parts together, then fix the legs to the body and finish with the head.

Once you have made the blank, then comes the pleasurable task of whittling the horse to shape. It's all pretty straightforward. All you do is round over the back of the neck and body, swiftly model the face and the hooves, trim the legs and so on. Of course, the degree of modeling will to a great extent depend upon your knowledge of horse anatomy. But that said, I believe that in the context of toys, the imagery is best stylized and simplified. Or to put it another way, yes, the horse needs to look like a horse, but at the same time you do have to be mindful that it needs to be strong.

With the overall horse whittled and sanded to shape, run a saw cut down the back of the neck and glue fix the little wooden pegs that go to make the mane. After a lot of trial and error, I found that a good method is to cut a couple wooden barbecue sticks into 1" lengths, slice the ends so that they are a tight push fit in the saw kerf, and then use cyanoacrylate to glue the sticks one at a time in the slots. When you are pleased with the shape and placing of the pegs, dribble a tad more glue along the whole row and, finally, trim them to length.

When you come to the tail, whittle it to shape as seen in the side view, and then whittle the shape as seen in the top view. It is a little bit tricky because the pine is relatively hard and grainy, but you don't have to get too fussed about the precise shape. Lastly, drill two holes in the horse—one for the tail and one for the wire. Then glue the tail into place.

Making the horse is pretty easy, but if you look closely at the photographs, you will see that I needed to correct various mistakes. For example, I needed to inset strips to strengthen the hooves, and I had to glue and dowel-pin one of the legs so as to strengthen the short grain. All I am saying is don't get in a sweat if a leg splits off or something else breaks. Just make a glue-and-peg repair and start over.

MAKING THE STAND AND THE COUNTERBALANCE BALL

The stand can be as plain or as fancy as the mood takes you. As long as the height and placing of the posts allow for the swing of the wire and the counterbalance ball, and the horizontal crossbar is level and parallel to the base, then the actual shape and construction are a matter for personal choice. I decided to go for a turned ring base, and whittled posts, crossbar and ball, but you could go for turned posts or other changes.

PUTTING IT TOGETHER

Once you have made the horse, the stand and the ball, then comes the frustrating and finger-twisting, but very enjoyable, task of putting it all together. Start by gluing the posts in the base and gluing and pinning the crossbar. Don't forget that the posts must be parallel and the crossbar level.

Now, having first drilled a hole in the horse's belly and flattened one end of the counterbalance wire, dribble glue in the hole on the underside of the horse and push the flattened end of the wire in place. This done, drill a hole right through the ball and thread the ball on the wire. Next, bend the wire into a gentle curve and position the horse on the crossbar. Try out various curves of wire until the horse is nicely balanced. Then glue the ball in place and clip off the excess wire. Finally, give all the surfaces a thin coat of varnish and let it dry. Burnish the whole thing with beeswax, and the horse is finished and ready for action.

MATERIALS LIST—PROJECT FIFTEEN

HORSE

A	Head (1)	1"×2"×2¼"
B	Body (2)	1½"×¾"×3½"
C	Legs (4)	½"×2"×3"
D	Tail (1)	⅝"×1"×3"
E	Wooden barbecue sticks (2)	⅛" diameter

STAND

F	Base (1)	1½"×6"×6"
G	Posts (2)	1"×1"×14"
H	Crossbar (1)	½"×⅞"×6½"

COUNTERBALANCE

I	Ball (1)	2"×2"×2" cube

HARDWARE AND EXTRAS

J	Wire coathanger (1)	16"
K	Screws and nails	various
L	Cyanoacrylate	

Note that all measurements allow for a small amount of cutting waste.

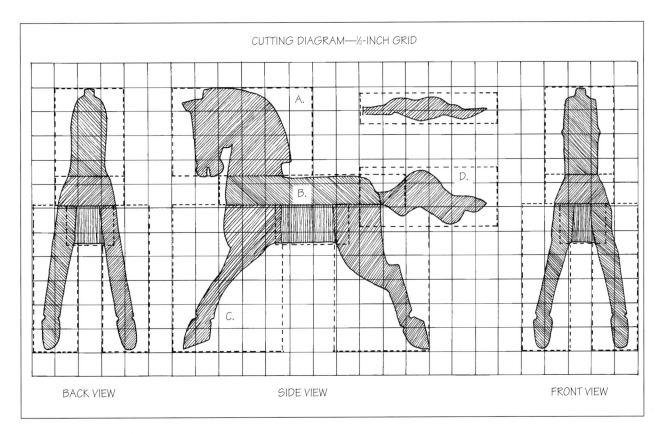

CUTTING DIAGRAM—½-INCH GRID

A.

B.

C.

D.

BACK VIEW   SIDE VIEW   FRONT VIEW

WORKING DRAWING B

SPECIAL TIP

Gill—my wife and better half—has just pointed out that there are toys for babies, toys for toddlers and toys for adults. She says that while the balancing horse is the perfect toy for an adult—you know the sort of thing, a toy that can be played with at the dinner table when kids, friends and family are looking on—it's not the sort of toy that you give to a boisterous five-year-old!

STEP-BY-STEP STAGES

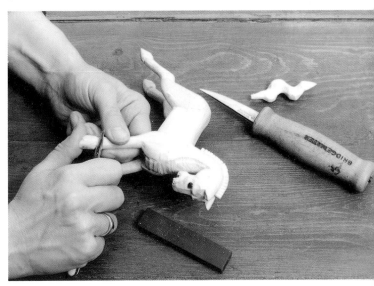

1 Having glued up the blank, use your knives to model the details. Use tightly controlled paring cuts, all the while being careful not to damage the relatively fragile short-grain areas like the ears. Note that I had a trial fitting of the eyes at this stage—I was eager to see how the overall image looked.

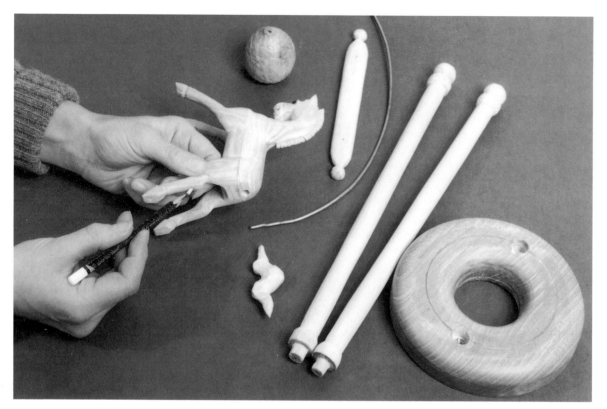

2 I had a bit of trouble when it came to the short grain on the back legs, so much so that I needed to reinforce one of them with a glued dowel. All I did was drill a hole across the run of the grain, dip a cocktail stick in glue and run it in the hole.

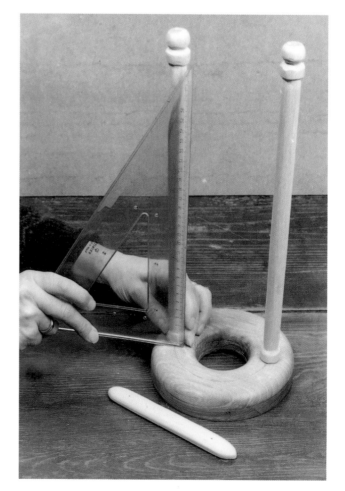

3 When you are gluing up, make sure that the posts are square to the base and parallel to each other. The good thing about using the PVA glue is that the long setting period allows you plenty of time to fiddle and fuss to get it right.

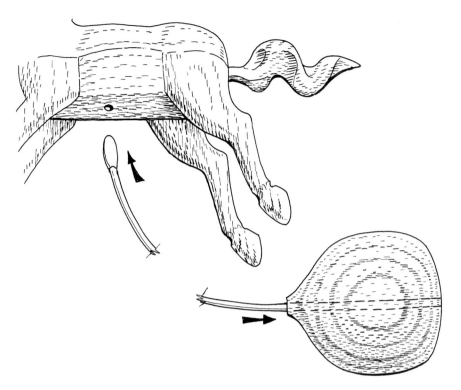

4 Flatten the end of the wire, smear it with glue, and then force it into the drilled hole (top). Having played around until the horse is more or less balanced, thread, glue and wedge the ball in place (bottom).

5 Finally, tweak the curve of the wire until the horse is perfectly posed.

DESIGN OPTION

Design for a single-seater galloper, circa 1895-1905, by J.R. Anderson.
We drew a good part of our inspiration for this project from this design.

INSPIRATION AND PERSPIRATION

We both love woodwork! I am particularly interested in totem poles, wooden masks, ships' figureheads, fairground horses, boxes, chests and medieval furniture. Gill enjoys toymaking, woodturning, chip-carved love tokens and chairmaking. If it is made of wood, then we are interested! Having written and illustrated more than thirty woodworking books, we are always asked how we search out the designs and ideas for our woodwork.

Well, the research for this project went something like this. We started by looking in the library and in old bookshops. Having searched out just about everything that was ever written on wooden toys, we then packed a huge lunch—lots of sandwiches and coffee, enough for a whole day—and drove to the nearest big-city museum. We looked at pre-twentieth-century ethnic toys, modern Third World toys, toys made in Europe, American folk art toys, toys made in Africa, and so on. While we were at

it, we also visited toyshops and galleries. We even visited a fairground museum. And along the way we collected photographs, made sketches, bought one or two toys, visited antique shops and fleamarkets, and generally did our level best to find out everything there is to know about the subject. For a week or so, we ate, slept and talked wooden toys. At the end of it all, I saw that this project draws its inspiration from English Victorian counterbalance toys, American fairground carousel horses, and American and European rocking horses—with all manner of little bits of this and that thrown in for good measure.

The good thing about researching projects in this way is that it gives us all sorts of ideas. Next time around I might make a fairground horse, or a balancing lady toy, or perhaps a large carved horse's head. Or maybe I could carve a horse plaque for our friend who has a stable, or a horse's head hitching post, or. . . .

DESIGN OPTION

Here's a head detail from a carousel horse circa 1926, Circus World, Orlando, Florida (top), and a horse from the Crescent Park carousel, circa 1895, Riverside, East Providence (bottom).

Old-Fashioned Push-Along Toys

RUNNING ROSY

A doll to kiss, a doll to cuddle—at some time or other, most of us have sought the cozy, clinging comfort of a toy doll. Running Rosy is something more than a doll. She's a sort of doll in a hurry, the perfect push-along-the-carpet plaything for younger kids. This is a beautiful plaything, a real delight for kids and adults alike. She's strong, easy to make, nicely rounded for "learning" hands, but best of all, her wheel-turning movement is just right for active toddlers who like to push toys along the floor.

If you are looking to make a unique toy for a unique kid, then this is the one.

MAKING THE TOY

When you have carefully studied the working drawings, take the tracing paper, a pencil, ruler and compass, and carefully set out the design on the wood. If you are going to stay with my choice of materials—plywood sandwiched between solid wood—then you need six cutouts in all: two solid wood outside body parts, two plywood head and body spacers, and two plywood foot-wheels. If you are wondering about my choice of materials, it's pretty straightforward and logical. While the head-and-body spacer and the wheel need to be strong in all directions across the grain, they also need to be safe for kids,

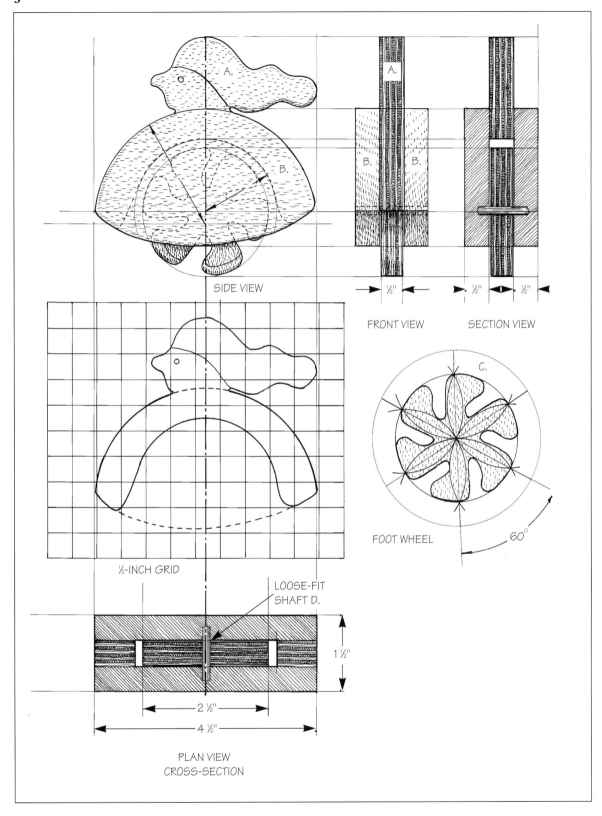

SIDE VIEW

FRONT VIEW   SECTION VIEW

½"   ½"   ½"

C.

FOOT WHEEL   60°

½-INCH GRID

LOOSE-FIT
SHAFT D.

1 ½"

2 ½"

4 ½"

PLAN VIEW
CROSS-SECTION

as well as relatively easy to work with a coping saw. All things considered, we thought that best-quality ¼″-thick multi-layer plywood was a winner on many counts. It's strong, it's stable, it's easy to cut, and it's easy to bond layers together to give extra strength.

When you have made all the cutouts, rub the two foot-wheels down to a smooth, round-edged finish—so that they are smooth to the touch and the total two-wheel thickness is something less than ½″. Next, establish the position of the pivotal dowel holes through the wheel and into the inside face of each solid wood body part. Then drill them out with a bit size that gives you a slightly loose fit for your chosen dowel.

To assemble: Glue one body part to one side of the central head-body spacer. Set the two foot-wheels in the cavity so that the feet are facing in the correct direction. Slide the dowel in place, and, lastly, glue the other body part in place so that the foot-wheels and pivotal dowel are nicely contained.

When the glue is dry, rub the whole works down so that the corners are rounded and good to hold. Aim for a form that is going to be safe and comfortable in a toddler's hands. Finally, use watercolors to tint in the imagery, give the whole works one or more coats of clear varnish, and the toy is finished.

SPECIAL TIP

Wooden toys must be childproof! Being mindful that toddlers are, at the very least, going to stick the toy in their mouths, it's most important that all the fixtures, fittings and materials be totally secure and nontoxic. Perhaps most important of all, the wood must be splinter resistant. With all this in mind, we chose to use multi-ply for the central layer and for the wheels, for the simple reason that it's easy to work, good to touch, strong across short grain "necks," and it glues and finishes well.

Don't think you can cut costs by using the coarse-centered plywood that goes by such names as "block ply," "stout heart" and "Malaysian." I say this because plywood of this type and character tends to be difficult to work, soft, almost impossible to sand to a good finish, and prone to splintering. No, when we say "multi-ply," we are specifically referring to the type of plywood that is built up in thin $\frac{1}{16}$″ layers or veneers. A plywood of this character has a smooth, white, close-grained face, it's tremendously strong and it's great to work. Ask for "best-quality, multi-ply, multilayer or multi-core plywood," and don't be talked into anything else.

Note, a sheet of ¼″-thick multilayer plywood should be made up of four or five thin veneer layers.

MATERIALS LIST—PROJECT SIXTEEN

A	Head-body spacer (2)	¼″×5″×5″ plywood
B	Outside body parts (2)	½″×3″×5″ solid wood
C	Foot-wheels (2)	¼″×3″×3″ plywood
D	Pivotal dowel (1)	¼″ dowel × 1¼″ long

Note that all measurements allow for a small amount of cutting waste.

HARDWARE AND EXTRAS
E Artist's watercolor paints—colors to suit
F Clear varnish

USING PLYWOOD

Best quality multi-ply is a first choice material for small cutout type toys. It is amazingly strong and it rubs down to a good smooth-to-touch finish.

STEP-BY-STEP STAGES

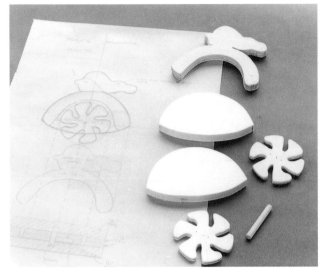

1 Check the component parts against the working drawings. And just in case you are wondering why I opted to use two ¼″ thicknesses to make up the ½″-thick spacer—rather than a single ½″ thickness—the simple answer is that I had lots of pieces of ¼″ ply that needed to be used up.

2 Fix the two wheels together with a piece of double-sided sticky tape and rub them down so that they are slightly less than ½″ in total thickness. The use of the tape not only ensures that both wheels are identical, it also makes them easier to handle.

3 Test the wheels in the body cavity. They need to be an easy loose-turning fit. Note that in this test run I have the feet running in the wrong direction!

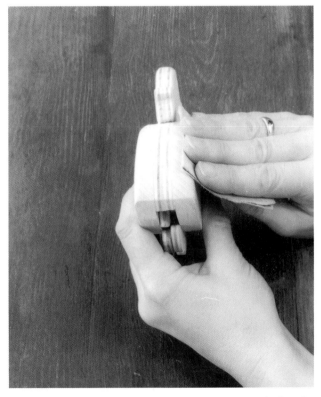

4 Rub the whole works down to a smooth finish. Close your eyes to test the finish—it's vital that every surface, edge and angle be supersmooth to the touch.

RUNNING REG IN HARDWOOD

Kids are so perceptive! When our Rosy toy was finished and up and running, I took it around to the 5-year-old girl next door for a bit of no-nonsense, in-depth criticism. Of course I was expecting a little bit of praise, but, oh no. All she said was, "But . . . where is running Reg?" So there you go, we had no other option but to make a Running Reg toy.

COUNTERCHANGE CUTTING

The clever thing about this project is not so much the design, but rather the way the two contrasting thicknesses of wood are cut and then counterchanged. It's an amazingly simple but subtle technique. All you do is sandwich two contrasting sheets of wood together, fret the design through both layers, and then swap the cutouts around so that the cutouts are contrasting.

PROCEDURE

Take the four pieces of wood—the sycamore, the mahogany, and the two pieces of plywood—and use the double-sided sticky tape to make a sandwich that has the plywood as the filling. When you are happy with the arrangement, carefully press transfer the traced imagery through to the sycamore side of the sandwich. Use the scroll saw to fret out the outside profile. This done, ease off the outside layers—the sycamore and the mahogany—and stick them together.

Cut out the plywood inner shape and the wheels as already described (see page 96). Then comes the very clever procedure of counterchange cutting. The method is beautifully simple. All you do is take the two profiles—the sycamore and the mahogany, all nicely stuck together with the double-sided tape—and saw them down into all the little parts that go to make up the design. For example, with this design I ran cuts through at either side of the hat band and under the chin. All you then do is swap the cutouts around and put the toy together in much the same way as already described.

MATERIALS LIST: OPTION

A (1) Prepared sycamore or maple wood—
$\frac{1}{2}$″ × 5″ × 6″

B (1) Prepared thick dark wood—I used a piece of salvaged mahogany—$\frac{1}{2}$″ × 5″ × 6″

C (2) Pieces of plywood—$\frac{1}{4}$″ × 5″ × 5″

HARDWARE AND EXTRAS

D PVA glue

E Yacht varnish

F Double-sided sticky tape

STEP-BY-STEP STAGES

1 Having fitted the very finest blade in the scroll saw, very carefully cut the design down into its component parts. It's important that you use a new, well-tensioned blade and go at it slowly, so that each and every cut is well placed and square to the wood.

2 Ease the layers apart, remove the double-sided tape and counterchange the parts. Note the little cut that goes to make the design of the mouth.

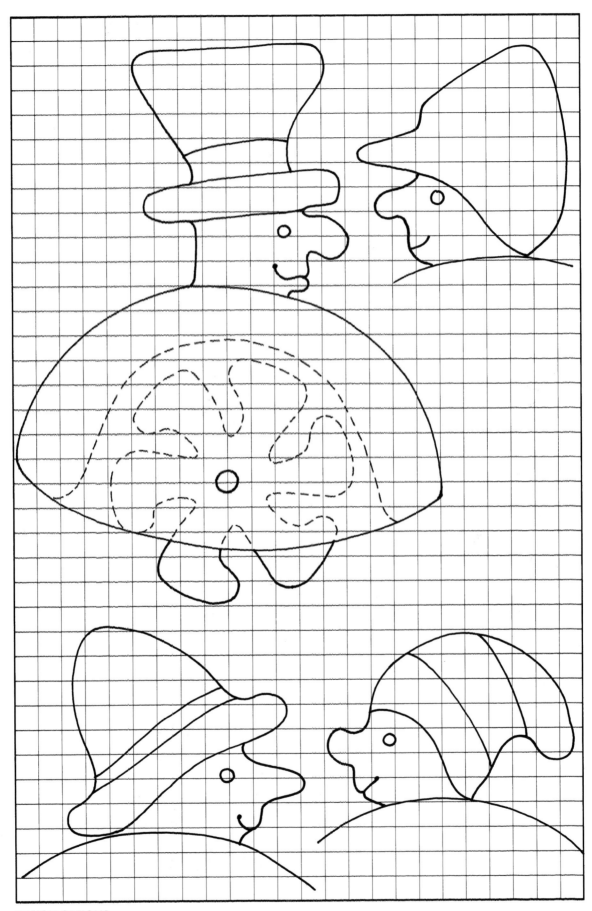

DESIGN OPTIONS

TOY SAFETY

Traditional wooden toys are enormous fun! Wood-workers like making them and kids like playing with them. But you do have to bear in mind that the average, intelligent finger-sticky toddler is generally going to do his level best to push the toy in his mouth and/or up his nose, if not worse! If you are going to make wooden toys, you have most certainly got to make sure that all the structures and all the materials are completely safe. If you are going to present the toys as gifts and/or make them for sale, you are legally bound to make sure that they are "safe, sound and fitting for their purpose." What this means is that you must ensure that every part of the toy is safe—no splinters, no toxic materials, no loose parts that can be swallowed. Be warned, ignorance is no excuse under the law—*you must make sure that everything is safe!* The following will provide you with some good sound guidelines.

Paint

Since kids like brightly colored toys, it's vital that you make sure that you use paints that are completely safe and nontoxic. Yes, your dad's old paint might still be in good condition, and, yes, it would give a wonderfully glossy, hard-wearing finish, but then again, it is almost certainly poisonous! Most old paints contain all manner of toxic mixes, everything from lead and antimony to arsenic. You must set out on the assumption that all old paints are dangerous.

When I asked around, I was assured that all modern paints are required by law to meet certain nontoxic, lead-free standards. But when I took it a bit further and phoned a paint manufacturer, they said that though their paints do most certainly come within safe standards, they don't necessarily come up to the standards required by the "Toy Safety" laws. As you can see, the whole area of paints and toy safety is somewhat difficult. I personally think that the best advice is either to use water stains and cover them with water-based varnish or to use acrylic paints. If you are concerned about paints and toy safety, then it's best if you write to various well-known paint manufacturers and ask their advice.

Wood Types

Although I have had no personal experience in this matter, I do understand that certain exotic wood types are dangerous if they are chewed. For example, I read of a case in which a child chewed a wooden toy from a Third World country, and the juices in the wood caused the child to go into some sort of shock. If we err on the side of safety and take it that some wood varieties are toxic, then the best advice is to use only wood varieties that we know to be safe. So, if we take it that modern American and British toymakers know what they are doing, it looks to me as if we should be going for wood types like lime, sycamore, beech, birch, oak and pine.

Fittings

As I remember, kids are always trying to pry their toys apart in an effort to find out how they work. This being the case, it's a good idea to avoid nails, small pieces of wire, and component parts that could in any way crack, splinter or shatter. The best advice is to use brass screws, glued dowels and glued layers.

Form

In many ways, the form a toy takes is as important as its substance and structure. For example, if a toy has a component part that is long, thin and spiky, or a part that could be swallowed, or a part that could be inserted into the ear or nose, then it follows that the toy in question has been badly designed. If and when you are designing your toys, or if you decide to modify this one, you must make sure that it's safe. For example, it might be a good idea to extend the walking girl's hair so as to make more of a handle, but the question is—would it be safe?

Turned Salt and Pepper Mills

Every once in awhile, a good project idea comes to me right out of the blue. And so it was one day when I was sitting down to dinner. I was fiddling around with our horrible diminutive, pressed plastic, difficult-to-hold salt and pepper mills, and trying to fill them for the umpteenth time, when the idea suddenly came to me—Eureka! I could make a couple of cone-shaped mills on the lathe—something really big, bold and sculptural, something that wouldn't need filling every ten minutes or so,

something that would be a joy to the eye as well as to the hand.

And that was how this project came into being. Okay, perhaps they aren't to everyone's taste and, yes, they are a bit on the big side—but they are certainly a unique conversation piece. The over-coffee chat usually goes something like, "Where did you get those er . . . big/strange/terrible/unusual/beautiful salt and pepper mills?"—ha!

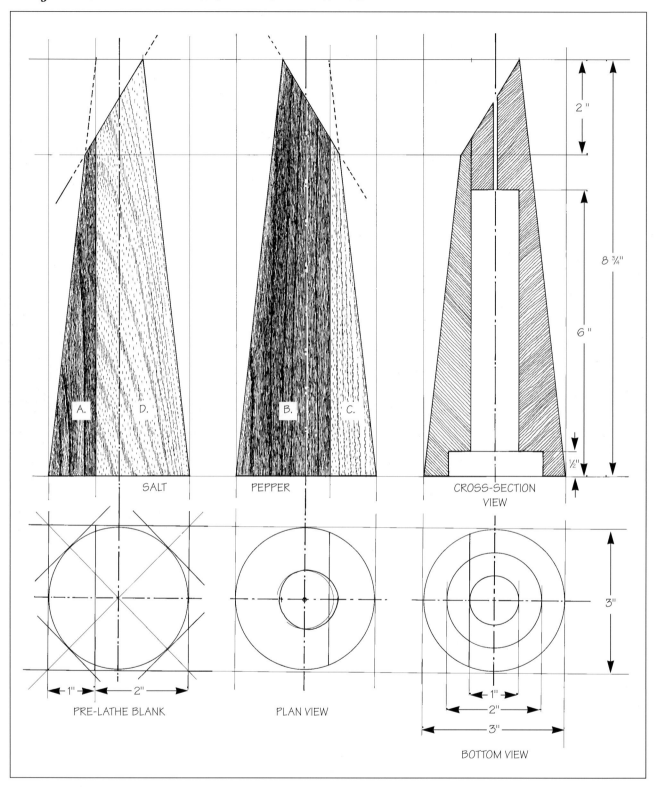

SALT

PEPPER

CROSS-SECTION
VIEW

PRE-LATHE BLANK

PLAN VIEW

BOTTOM VIEW

2"

8 ¾"

6"

½"

3"

1"

2"

3"

1"

2"

A.

D.

B.

C.

MAKING THE SALT AND PEPPER MILLS

When you have studied the project and generally brought your lathe and tools to order, take your chosen wood and cut it to size. You need four 10″ lengths in all: one dark and one light 1¼″×3″, and one dark and one light 2¼″×3″.

Plane the mating faces and glue and clamp them together so that you have two 3″×3″-square sections. If you have done it right, the two blocks will be color counterchanged, so that one is predominantly dark with a light strip and the other visa versa. You can, of course, glue the wood up from larger section material—so that you have a single large lump—and then slice it down to size.

First establish the end centers of the blocks. Scribe out 3″-diameter circles and clear the bulk of the waste so that you more or less have octagonal sections. Then mount the wood on the lathe and swiftly turn it down to a 3″-diameter smooth, round section. With the workpiece held securely in the four-jaw chuck and pivoted on the tailstock center, take the dividers and mark off the total 8¾″ length. Take the parting tool and sink a tool-width channel at each end. Run the tool in to a depth of 1″ so that you are left with a 1″-diameter core at each end of the turning. Now, with the narrow end of the cone nearest the chuck, take the gouge and make repeated passes from right through to left.

When you have made the cone shape, carefully part the waste off at the tailstock end. With the drill chuck mounted in the tailstock, run two holes into the wide end of the cone—first a 2″-diameter hole at about ½″ deep, followed up by a 1″-diameter hole at about 5″ to 6″ deep.

Finally, part the cone off from the lathe, run a 3/32″-diameter hole down into the top of the cone at top center, and saw off the top of the cone so that it is truncated at an angle. Rub down to a smooth finish and then burnish with a small amount of vegetable oil.

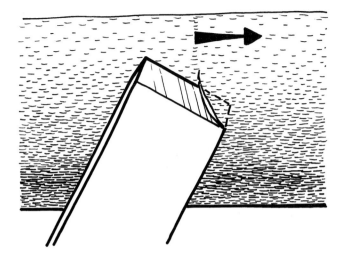

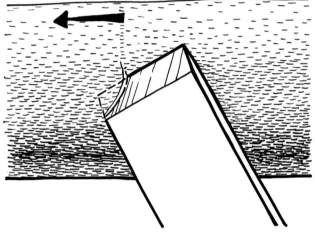

TOOL TIP

When you are using a turning chisel, the procedure is to lift the handle up until the lower end of the cutting edge begins to bite, then advance the cut in the direction of the blade. If you work in this way, you will find that the skewed approach greatly minimizes tool pressure and consequent flexing of the workpiece.

MATERIALS LIST—PROJECT SEVENTEEN

A Dark wood (1) 1¼″×3″×10″—we used American Walnut

B Dark wood (1) 2¼″×3″×10″

C Light wood (1) 1¼″×3″×10″—we used English Hornbeam

D Light wood (1) 2¼″×3″×10″

HARDWARE AND EXTRAS

E Corks or plastic stoppers to fit the 1″-diameter holes

SPECIAL TIP

Because the gist of this project has to do with being able to drill deep, accurate, smooth-sided holes, I would always advise using either a Forstner bit or a saw tooth multi-spur-type bit. As to the actual drilling procedure, if you have to do it off the lathe—say on a drill press—then be warned, if you go off center, there is a big chance that you might break through the walls of the cone.

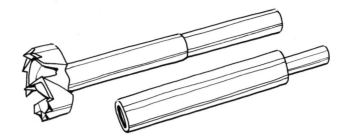

DRILLING HOLES ON THE LATHE

If you need to drill holes on the lathe, then it's best to get a Forstner or multispur bit with an extension bar.

STEP-BY-STEP STAGES

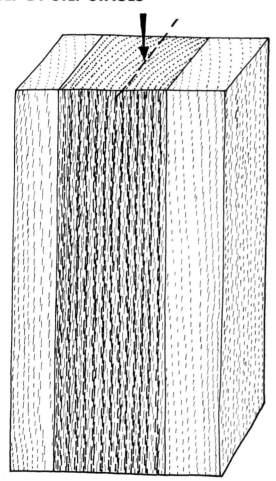

1 If you don't like the notion of gluing up small individual strips of wood or you are working with bigger pieces, a very economical method is to glue up the three blocks as shown, and then saw the resultant piece through from end to end.

2 If you are working on a small lathe, it's always a good idea to clear the bulk of the waste by planing the wood to an octagonal section. You need to finish up with two blanks, one predominantly light and the other predominantly dark.

3 In the interest of safety, you must make absolutely sure that the laminations are sound and well glued. If you have any doubts at all, it's best to start over. Be warned, if ever you should decide to modify this project and go for different light-dark proportions—meaning a different gluing-up arrangement—you must make sure that the lamination line occurs well clear of the center of spin. If you don't, there is a danger that the tailstock point will force the wood apart.

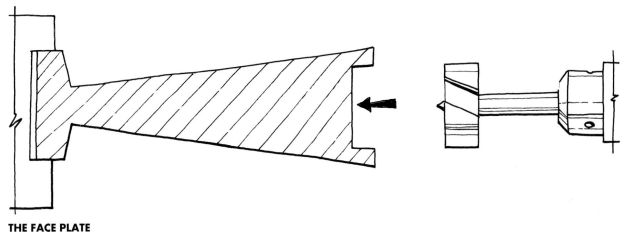

THE FACE PLATE
Using a faceplate is a good, sound means of securing a large blank. Notice the use of short, fat screws for maximum holding efficiency.

4 With the workpiece held secure in the jaws of the chuck, fit a 2″-diameter Forstner bit in the tailstock chuck and run a ½″-deep hole into the end of the cone.

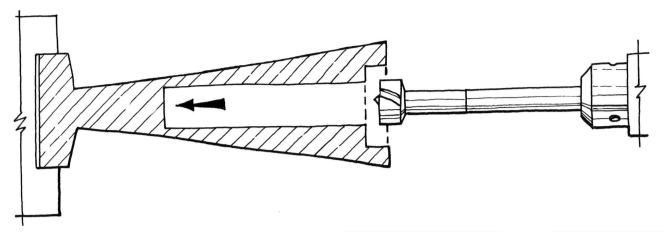

5 Having made the 2″-diameter hole, follow up with a 1″ bit and sink a hole to a depth of about 5″, ½″ at a time. The procedure is, run the bit in ½″ and then back out, and then back in another ½″, and so on, so that you remove the waste little by little and give the bit a chance to cool off.

7 Having drilled the ³⁄₃₂″-diameter hole down into the top of the cone—right through to the cavity—and used a fine-tooth backsaw to truncate the cone, use the graded sandpapers to achieve a smooth finish.

6 The drilled and recessed base allows you to fit all manner of corks and plugs. If you like the idea of the project but want to go for something a little more sophisticated, then many specialist suppliers stock small brass screw-stopper-and-collar units that can easily be fitted into the recess.

GRINDING MILLS

Traditional Colonial-style salt and pepper mills are fascinating! It's not so much the way they fit together and operate—although this is very interesting in itself—but the way they are made. There is something really exciting about the procedure. One moment you have a couple of lumps of wood and the next you have two little machines. Really good fun!

THE PROCEDURE

Having first made sure that the wood is free from splits and cavities, mount it on the lathe and swiftly turn the greater part of the length down to a 2¼″-diameter cylinder. Run guidelines around the cylinder so that the top part of the mill is nearest to the tailstock end of the lathe.

Turn the top of the mill—called a capstan—to shape and very carefully part off. Fit the tailstock drill chuck, set the 1⅛″-diameter Forstner bit in the chuck, and run a hole into the end of the cylinder. Sink the hole in to a depth of about 3″. Part off the 5¼″-long cylinder.

Wind the tailstock up so that the remaining short length of wood is well supported. Turn off a spigot that is going to be a tight push fit in the 1⅛″-diameter hole that you have drilled into what will be the top end of the body. Now, slide the body onto the spigot, refit the tailstock drill chuck and bore different size holes into what will be the base of the mill body. Bore the first hole at 1½″-diameter and ½″ deep, followed up by the second hole at 1⅛″-diameter and as deep as it will go.

When you are this far, the rest is easy. You simply reverse the body of the mill in the chuck—so that the base is in the chuck—fit the capstan on the mill, and then wind up the tailstock and turn the mill to shape.

MATERIALS LIST: OPTION

A (2) 2½″ × 2½″ × 12″ pieces of beech

B (2) 7½″-long mechanisms—one for salt and the other for pepper

STEP-BY-STEP STAGES

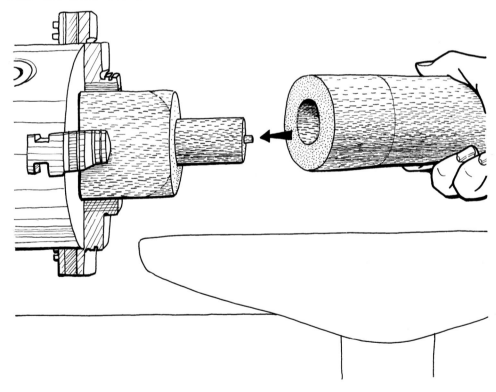

1 Having turned the capstan to shape and parted off, drill a 1⅛″-diameter hole into what will be the top of the body. Then push the cylinder onto the spigot.

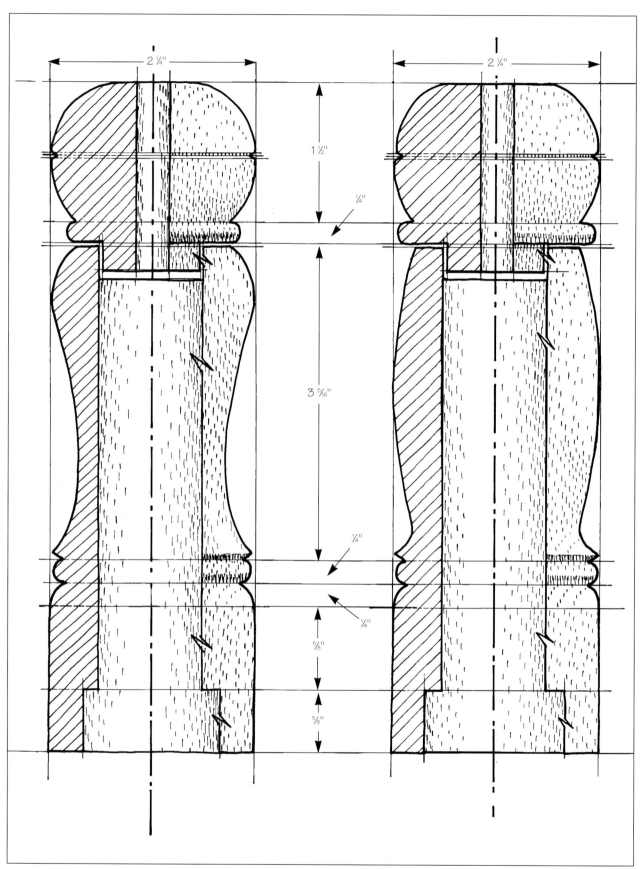

WORKING DRAWING B

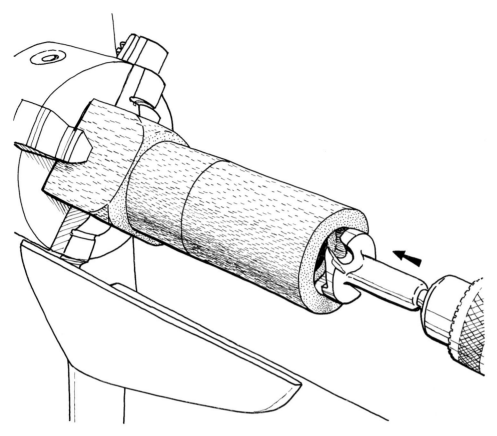

2 Bore two holes into the bottom of the mill—the first hole at 1½″ in diameter and ½″ deep, followed by the second hole at 1⅛″ in diameter and as deep as it goes.

3 Having more or less turned the capstan to shape, fit it in the chuck and bring it to a good finish. Run a ⅜″-diameter hole through the workpiece.

4 Fit the whole works back on the lathe and sand and burnish to a good smooth finish.

5 Slide the mill mechanism up through the body and fix with the little bar and a couple of screws.

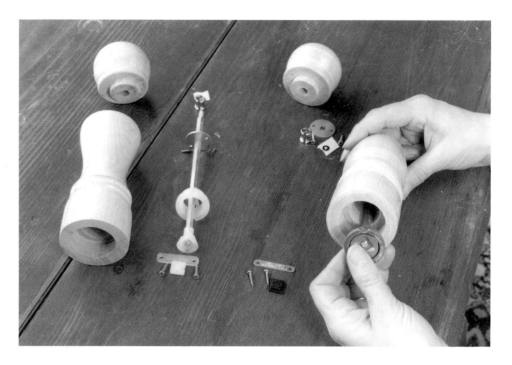

6 Having screwed the ring washer on the capstan spigot, slide the capstan on the threaded rod and fit with the fancy head screw.

DESIGNING FOR THE LATHE

Designing for the lathe is uniquely problematic. The success of the design not only hinges on aesthetics and function but also on the turning techniques. Of course, the same goes when you are designing a chair or whatever—you still have to make decisions about the tools and the techniques—but with turning, the tools and the techniques are paramount. Also, the design solution is very closely related to method. In chairmaking, the balance of concern is perhaps equally distributed between aesthetics, function and technique; with wood turning, the technique concerns far outweigh all others. In fact, when I'm designing for the lathe, my big worry is not whether it looks good or if it functions. Rather, I'm concerned with how I will hold, secure and approach the workpiece while it is being turned, and whether it is safe.

When I'm designing for wood turning, I always run through the following little how-will-I-do-it checklist:

■ Is the lathe powerful enough? Will the motor size happily shift the weight of the wood?

■ Is the distance between centers long enough to accommodate the design?

■ Is the radius of swing big enough? (Meaning, is the distance between the center of spin and the top of the bed great enough?)

■ How am I going to hold the wood? Am I going to use the four-jaw chuck, the face plate, the screw chuck, the pronged center, or what?

■ Will I turn multiples in one piece to be cut apart or as individual units?

■ Will I need to use a drill chuck in the tailstock mandrel?

■ Will I need to use special drill bits with extension pieces?

■ Will I turn the item over the bed of the lathe? Or will I use the outboard bowl-turning option on the back of the lathe?

■ Is the chosen wood type available in the size and quality I need? Will I need to laminate up?

■ Is the wood the traditional choice for a turning of this size and character?

■ Will I need to use special tools other than the usual scrapers, chisels and gouges?

As you can see, at least half of the design procedure has to do with the lathe and related tooling. Of course, just about all your questions are answered if you want to turn something like a baseball bat—your only worry is length—but if the turning is more complex with maybe two component parts that fit together, then it's not so easy and needs thinking about.

Let's say, for example, that you have set yourself the design problem of turning a large lidded container—the biggest diameter possible on your lathe—a form about as high as it is round. The first thing you do is measure the radius of swing and double it. If your lathe measures 3″ from the center of the headstock down to the top face of the bed, you can reckon on a diameter of no more than 6″. So, you are turning a container about 6″ in diameter and 6″ high.

Next, you have to decide how the block of wood is to be held and the order of work. Though there are many

ways of proceeding, I usually turn the wood down between centers—meaning the outside profile—then hold the wood in the four-jaw chuck while I hollow-turn the center. When I have cleared the waste from inside the container and maybe turned the rim, I then change the container around on the chuck—so that it is held by its rim—and finish up by turning the base.

What else to say, except that you must always think well ahead before you put tools to wood. And of course, as with all potentially dangerous machinery, you must always be wide awake and ready for the unexpected.

Folk Art Pipe Box

I wonder why our great-great-great-grandparents put such a huge amount of energy and enthusiasm into making pieces of woodwork that were used for everyday chores. Okay, so they had to have such functional items as dough troughs, candle boxes and flour bins. But remembering that every stick of wood had to be laboriously cut, planed, fretted and finished by hand, why did they put extra time and trouble into decorating their woodwork with so many fancy curlicues?

If you want to try your hand at a piece of woodwork that perfectly illustrates this point, then this pipe box is for you. Inspired by an English eighteenth-century folk art original, boxes of a similar type, design and construction can be found all over—in England, in Wales, in Scotland, in America—in fact, just about anyplace people smoked long-stemmed clay pipes. The design of the box is beautifully fitting for its task. The pipes fit in the top half of the box, the "makings" fit in the little drawer, and the whole works hangs on the wall alongside the fireplace.

As to the fancy compass-worked edge design, it can be found on all kinds of eighteenth- and nineteenth-century woodwork—on everything from overmantel and cupboard shelves to bench trim, door surrounds and plate racks.

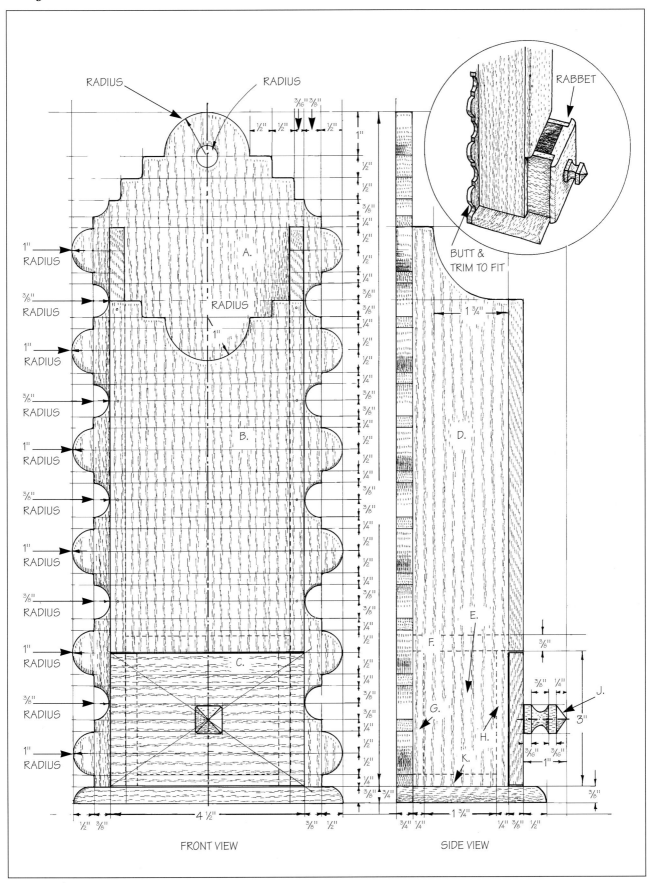

FRONT VIEW

SIDE VIEW

MAKING THE PIPE BOX

Having set the wood out with all the dip-and-arch curves, fret out the design.

When you have made all the component parts and pencil labelled them so there is no doubting what goes where and how, then comes the tricky, sticky-finger task of putting the box together. I found that the best way to work was to drill, pin and glue the components in the following order: (1) the main backing board to the main baseboard; (2) the side boards to the backing board; (3) the inside-box piece that forms the bottom to the pipe part of the box; (4) the front to the box. And lastly, I glued, pinned and adjusted the little drawer to fit the box.

When you come to the little drawer knob, all you do is trim a ¾″×¾″-square section of wood down to shape and plug it into a drilled hole.

Finally, when the glue is completely dry, trim and shape all the rough edges to a slightly rounded finish, give the whole works a rubdown with the finest-grade sandpaper, and then lay on a thin coat of wax or varnish.

MATERIALS LIST—PROJECT EIGHTEEN

BOX

A	Back board (1)	⅜″×6¼″×15½″—we used English oak throughout
B	Front board (1)	⅜″×4½″×7⅞″
C	Side boards (2)	⅜″×2¼″×12½″
D	Drawer sides (2)	¼″×3″×2¼″
E	Inside-box bottom (1)	⅜″×2¼″×3¾″
F	Drawer back (1)	¼″×3″×3¼″
G	Drawer front (1)	⅝″×3″×4½″
H	Box base (1)	⅜″×3⅛″×6¼″
I	Knob (1)	⅝″×⅝″×1⅝″
J	Drawer base (1)	¼″×2″×3¼″

Note that all measurements are to the mark—meaning they make no allowance for cutting waste.

HARDWARE AND EXTRAS

K Copper panel pins

L PVA glue

SPECIAL TIP

If you have a good close-up look at museum boxes of this character, you will see that a good part of the charm has to do with the choice of wood and the degree of finish. For example, while a good native wood looks beautifully fresh and understated—something like cherry, maple, pine or oak is just perfect—a fancy wood like mahogany or one of the exotic African woods tends to look too precious or "overdressed."

STEP-BY-STEP STAGES

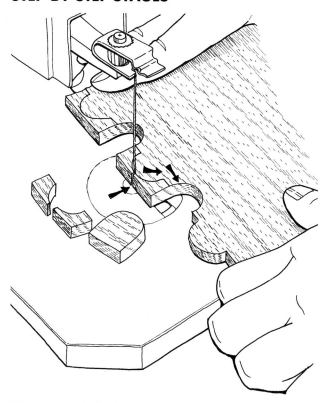

1 To work the fancy edge, start by cutting out all the deep concave **U** shapes—along the whole length of the wood—and then fret out the remaining convex forms. If you look at the arrows, you will notice that I always work in the direction of the grain—that is, two cuts that run down-and-out from the peak of the little bridge shape.

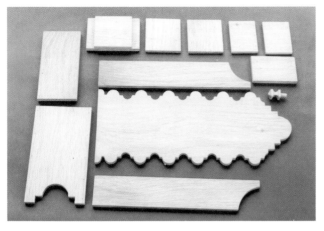

2 Having made all the component parts, pencil label them so that you know precisely how they fit one to another. If one side of a part is more attractive, or damaged, then now is the time to make decisions as to its placing.

3 Do a trial fitting to make sure that you haven't made any mistakes. Test for the squareness of the butting edges and mark in the position of the nail/panel pin holes.

5 Here's the finished drawer—all glued, pinned and rubbed down. Putting the drawer together is a little bit tricky, not because any single cut is complicated, but because the total form needs to be true, square and a good fit.

4 Do a trial fitting of the sides of the box and the sides of the drawer. If necessary, you can trim back the rabbet and/or the thickness of the wood. Establish the position of the drawer pull by marking with crossed diagonals.

Laminated Jewelry Box

This project draws its inspiration from the English decorative woodworking technique known as Tunbridgeware. This ware is characterized by small items that give the appearance of being worked with delicate tessera inlay. The technique involves gluing colored sticks of wood together in bundles and then repeatedly slicing, repositioning and re-gluing.

With this little box, the slicing and laminating technique is used in conjunction with what has come to be called "band saw joinery."

MAKING THE LAMINATED BOX

First and foremost, you have to understand that with this project there are several steps along the way where there is a high risk of the whole thing falling to pieces. This being so, we decided at the outset to work on two boxes at the same time, just in case of mistakes. Well, as you can see in the photographs, we got so far with one box and—Splap!—it came to grief.

When you have studied the working drawings, gather your chosen offcuts, and plane them down to smooth-sided sections. Stick them together side by side, like a long fence. When the glue is dry, plane both sides of the fence, cut it into short lengths, and then re-glue the resultant lengths into a layered sandwich. Continue slicing, planing, gluing and laminating, until you have what you consider an interesting multicolored brick. And of course, the more you slice and laminate, the smaller the design and the greater the complexity of the pattern.

Plane your brick to size so that it is $2\frac{1}{2}'' \times 2\frac{3}{4}''$ in section and 4″ long, with all six sides being smooth and at right angles to each other. Pencil label the various sides "top," "bottom," "back," "front," "left side" and "right side."

Use the band saw to cut a $\frac{1}{4}''$ slice from the "top" and "bottom," label the slices and put them carefully to one side. This done, set the shape of the drawer out on the rough face of the block, and use either a fine-bladed band saw or a scroll saw to cut it out. Next, slice the bottom off the drawer, label it and put it to one side. Then use the scroll saw to clear away the waste from what will be the inside of the drawer. While the saw is handy, cut away the two finger holes and run a cut straight down back-center of the shell-like piece that wraps around the drawer.

When you have made all six component parts—the top and bottom slabs of the brick, the all-in-one-piece back and sides that has been cut into two halves, the

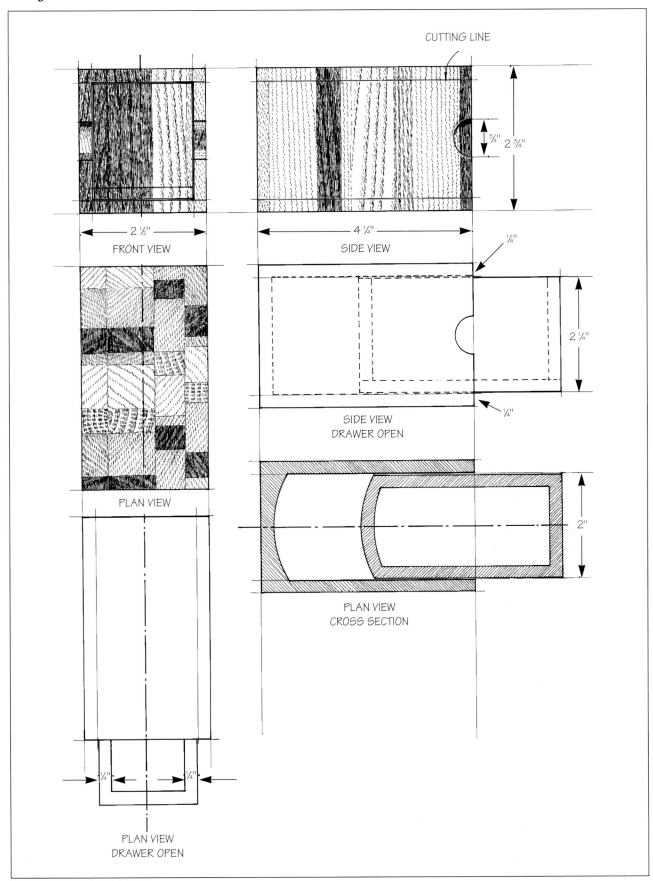

CUTTING LINE

¾" 2 ¾"

2 ½"

FRONT VIEW

4 ¼"

SIDE VIEW

¼"

2 ¼"

¼"

SIDE VIEW
DRAWER OPEN

PLAN VIEW

2"

PLAN VIEW
CROSS SECTION

¼"   ¼"

PLAN VIEW
DRAWER OPEN

drawer with the inside cut away, and the bottom to the drawer—take the finest-grade sandpaper and rub all the sides and faces down to a smooth finish. Be careful that you don't blur the corners.

To put the little box together, start by gluing the base onto the drawer. Then smear glue on mating faces and reconstruct the block so that the drawer is nicely and closely contained. Finally, when the glue is dry, sand and finish the box.

SPECIAL TIP

If you like the idea of this project and want to try something a little more complex, you could experiment with cross-laminating. For example, you could turn the slices around at the sandwiching steps so that all faces of the brick show end grain. Then again, you could try swapping and turning the bottom and side slices of the box so that the block pattern becomes even more complex and staggered.

STEP-BY-STEP STAGES

1 When you have made the block—all well glued and sawed to size—sand all the faces down to a smooth finish. Do your best to keep the corners crisp and at right angles.

MATERIALS LIST—PROJECT NINETEEN	
Box	A selection of contrasting offcuts all sawed and planed—we used American walnut, oak, cherry and tulipwood—at about ½″ thick and at various widths.

2 Saw slices off the top and bottom of the block and cut out the shape that goes to make the drawer. Be mindful that the drawer surround—meaning the piece that you see me holding—is very fragile at this stage and liable to break apart at the corners.

3 Put the component parts back together and label each and every face and mating edge, so there is no doubting how the parts fit one to another.

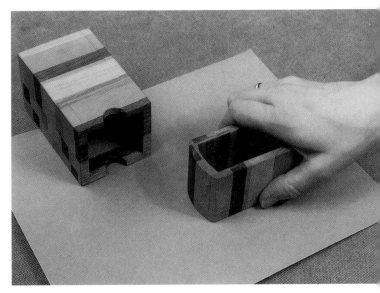

4 Having sliced off the bottom of the drawer block, saw out the inside-drawer waste and then glue the base back on the drawer. And just in case you have noticed that this photograph shows another block, the sad truth is the original block fell to bits when I was cutting the drawer. I think the problem was that I was a bit anxious and heavy-handed, and the glue hadn't quite cured.

5 Sanding the various faces is a very slow business for the simple reason that you have to work slowly and with care. You have to be most careful that you don't put undue pressure on the drawer—no squeezing the sides together.

6 If you find that the drawer is a somewhat loose fit, it's a good idea to give the inside of the box a couple of coats of sealer and then sand back to a nice push fit. The best procedure is to sand a little and test the fit, then sand some more, and so on until you are satisfied.

7 Sand the finger holes to a rounded finish. You have a choice at this stage . . . do you want to round and blur all the corners, or do you want to keep them sharp?

Marquetry Mirror

About five years ago, my son Glyn made a marquetry mirror for an English magazine called the *Woodworker*. It was a real success and there was lots of interest. This mirror draws its inspiration from that project. At first glance, this mirror appears to involve an incredibly complex and fine marquetry technique—very fine hairline inlays and a multitude of cuts. Certainly it is a most delicate and exquisite item, but appearances are not always what they seem! The marquetry surface is, in fact, made up from a sheet of specially printed and pressed flexible veneer, while the hairline inlay is made from strips of sycamore veneer glued to the kerf face. As to the technique, it's no more than a few saw cuts and a bit of ironing.

For the actual shape and character of the mirror, there are any number of exciting possibilities. You can chop and change the veneer around to create different effects; you can rearrange the saw cuts so that the little "window" is triangular, hexagonal or star-shaped. In fact, you can go for just about any shape that takes your fancy.

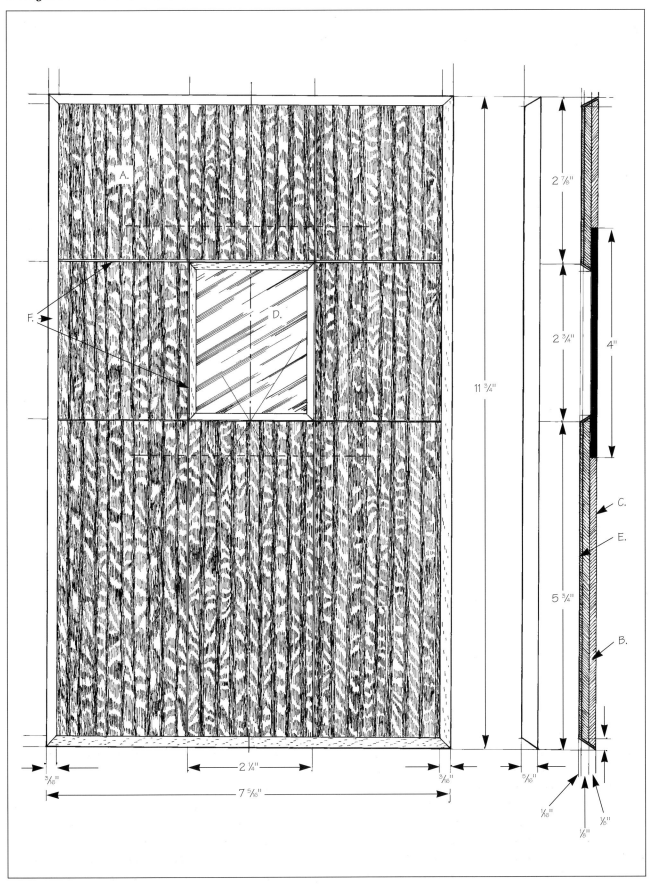

A.

F.

D.

2 ⁷⁄₈"

2 ³⁄₄"

4"

11 ³⁄₄"

C.

E.

5 ³⁄₄"

B.

³⁄₁₆"

2 ¹⁄₄"

³⁄₁₆"

⁵⁄₁₆"

7 ⁵⁄₁₆"

¹⁄₁₆"

¹⁄₈"

¹⁄₈"

MAKING THE MIRROR

Before you do anything else, you need to play around with the materials—the flexible veneer and the gluefilm. The gluefilm is wonderfully easy to use. All you do is position it paper-side up on the baseboard and iron it in place with a hot iron; remove the backing paper and position the marquetry on the gluefilm; cover the assembly with the backing paper and run the hot iron back and forth until the glue has melted.

When you understand how the gluefilm technique works, clear the bench ready for action. Start by cutting the two boards to size—the top board and the mirror thickness board. Then use the gluefilm to bond your chosen flexible veneer to the front face of the top board. And just in case you are wondering, yes, it is as easy as it sounds!

Having used a pencil, ruler and square to draw the lines of the design on the veneered surface so that they run off the edge of the board, sit awhile and consider your next move. As you can see, all you need to do is make four cuts straight across the board and at a mitered angle of 30°. Then fill the resultant saw-cut kerfs with a glued strip of veneer so that the angled veneer becomes the beveled edge.

Now there are two ways forward. You can either do as we do and make one cut straight down the length of the board, fill the cut up with the veneer strip and move onto the next cut, or you can make all four cuts and then fiddle about gluing up the whole assembly. Either way, the gluing procedure is the same.

■ Use the scroll saw to make the beveled cut across the board.

■ Use the gluefilm to bond the strip of sycamore veneer to one face of the kerf bevel.

■ Smear PVA glue on the face of the sycamore strip and push the other side of the board in place.

Then continue making beveled cuts with the scroll saw, sticking veneer strip to one side of the bevel, sticking the other side of the board in place, and then on to the next cut until the task is done. The trick is to finish up with a mirror hole that is nicely beveled on all four edges.

When the glue is dry, use a small plane and the finest-grade sandpaper to clean the whole works down to a smooth finish so that the edges of the veneer strips appear as fine inlay lines. This done, glue the two boards together to make the recess for the mirror tile. Finally, miter the edge of the two-board thickness, trim it with the veneer strip, burnish the whole works with beeswax polish, and the project is finished.

SPECIAL TIP

To my way of thinking, the whole art and craft of working with veneers has been revolutionized by the introduction of two miracle products: printed and pressed flexible veneer, and iron-on gluefilm. If you have trouble obtaining one of the products, don't be tempted to use traditional veneer and hot-melt glue, but rather visit a specialist supplier and ask specifically for the products by generic name. You need "thermoplastic gluefilm," and "pressed and printed flexible veneer." Flexible veneers come in a whole range of designs and colors, everything from imitations of exotic veneers to designs that look as if they have been woven.

MATERIALS LIST—PROJECT TWENTY

A	Front board (1)	1/8" ply ×7 5/16" ×11 3/4"
B	Mirror thickness board (1)	1/8" ply (same thickness as the mirror tile) ×7 5/16" ×11 3/4"
C	Backing paper (1)	6" ×6"—sticky-back paper or plastic to hold the mirror secure
D	Mirror tile (1)	4" ×4"-square tile
E	Veneer (1)	printed and pressed flexible veneer 12" ×12"—this allows for cutting waste
F	Inlay (1)	sycamore veneer 14" ×10"—this allows for a good amount of cutting waste

HARDWARE AND EXTRAS

G	Thermoplastic gluefilm (1)	18" ×18"
H	PVA glue	

STEP-BY-STEP STAGES

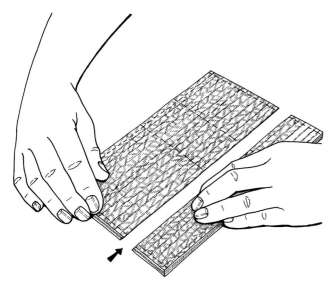

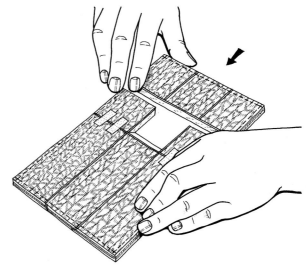

1 Set the saw table to a tilt angle of 30° and run a saw cut right across the length of the board. Then, glue a strip of veneer on the sawed edge and glue the two parts of the board back together.

2 Continue running straight saw cuts across the board and filling the kerf with veneer until the design is complete. If you do it right, the procedure will automatically result in the mitered edges of the mirror hole or window being veneered with the strip.

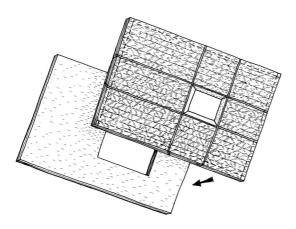

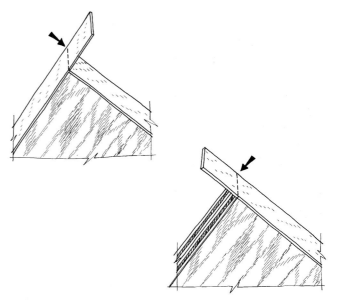

3 Glue the backing board in place so that you have the thickness of two boards. Then run a beveled cut around all four sides of the frame.

4 Glue the strips around the mitered edges and trim and sand the corners to a crisp finish.

MORE ABOUT THE CRAFT OF MARQUETRY AND INLAY

If you have enjoyed this project and want to know more about the craft of inlay and marquetry, then the following brief history will give you some useful leads.

Marquetry and inlay were originally inspired by the ancient craft of "intarsia"—the making of mosaics by the inlaying of precious and exotic materials into and/or onto a groundwork of solid wood. The Egyptians decorated much of their woodwork with inlay. In fact, in the tomb of the Egyptian king Tutankhamen, just about all the furniture is covered with an inlay made up of little briquettes of wood, gold and ivory.

Through the centuries, in Egypt, Rome, Persia, Japan and right across Europe, the craft of inlaying gradually evolved, with rich patrons employing craftsmen to painstakingly cover base woods with rare and exotic woods. The craft involved importing rare woods, slicing the wood into little chunks, and then setting the chunks or briquettes one at a time into the base wood. The process of inlay was massively expensive in time and materials.

And so it might have continued had not some tired and weary woodworker—sometime toward the end of the sixteenth century—invented the jigsaw. From then on, the whole process became swifter and more efficient, until about the beginning of the seventeenth century, when the technique became so improved and refined that woodworkers were using thin sheets of wood—by this time called veneer—to glue directly to the base wood.

The craft as we now know it can be divided into four areas of study—veneering, parquetry, boulle marquetry and window marquetry.

Veneering

In simple terms, the craft of veneering has to do with covering base wood with a more attractive species, to fool the eye into believing that the piece of furniture or other item is made of more expensive wood. Though at one time this area of the craft fell into disrepute, with the term "veneer" coming to mean tricky and/or cheap, it is now seeing a revival. Current thinking is that one way of saving rare and precious tree species is to make a little go a long way. For example, it is now possible to build a whole piece of furniture from a man-made sheet-wood material like MDF (medium density fiberboard), and then cover it with a pressed-and-printed flexible veneer—as in this project—or with plastic veneers or thin sheets of rare wood. One look through a batch of current woodworking magazines will bear out the fact that the time is fast coming when some woods will be so rare and costly that woodworkers will have no choice but to use thin decorative veneers on base-wood grounds. Interesting isn't it!

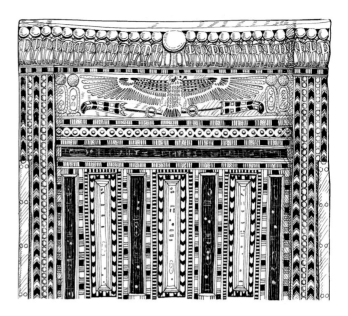

EGYPTIAN INLAY

Detail from the back of Tutankhamen's ceremonial chair—inlayed with exotic woods and precious stones.

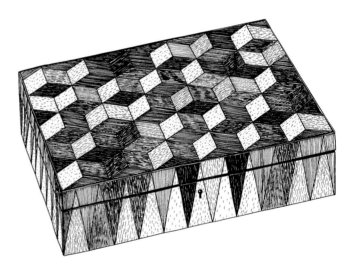

NINETEENTH-CENTURY PARQUETRY

A classic example of a parquetry box—made in Tunbridge Wells, England, in the middle of the nineteenth century.

Parquetry

Squares, checkerboards, counterchanges, triangles, diamonds and zigzags—parquetry is the art and craft of math, geometry and the straight line. While marquetry involves pictures, patterns and all manner of wavy-line imagery, parquetry concentrates on straight lines and geometrical patterns.

Many American marquetry craftsmen think of parquetry as being similar to fabric patchwork. It's a good comparison. If you think of the geometrical patterns that make up a quilt, and if you go on to think of this same pattern in terms of tiles of veneer spread out over a piece of furniture, or maybe over a floor, then you have a parquetry. If you enjoy playing around with rulers and set squares, and if you enjoy logic, order and straight, crisp lines, then you will enjoy parquetry.

Boulle Marquetry

Boulle is a type of marquetry that was popular in France in the seventeenth and eighteenth centuries. The technique was named after André Charles Boulle, a French marquetry craftsman under King Louis XIV. Now known as boulle, boule, or even, buhl, the technique might best be described as getting two designs for the price of one.

Traditionally, the boulle technique involves setting two thin sheets of contrasting material together—usually brass and an exotic wood—and then cutting through both sheets at the same time to create a number of pairs of identical cutouts. For example, if you have two sheets of veneer sandwiched together—one black and the other white—and you cut a circle shape through both sheets and then swap the cutouts around, you will have a black sheet with a white circle at its center and a white sheet with a black circle. If you were to continue cutting out more complex shapes and swapping them around, you would finish up with two identical counterchanged designs—one white on black and the other black on white. If you sandwich four sheets of veneer together, then the technique really begins to lift off. If you enjoy intricate sawing, and exquisite pattern work—say on small boxes and the like—and if you like the notion of using up every last piece of veneer, then perhaps this is a technique that you need to explore.

Window Marquetry

Window marquetry, sometimes called picture marquetry, involves pencil-press, transferring the design through to a sheet of scrap veneer, then cutting out the elements of the design one step at a time and replacing them with more decorative veneers.

For example, if you draw a picture of an old sailing ship on the scrap veneer and cut out, say, one of the sails so that you have a hole, then you can slide the hole over your choice veneer and try out various grain patterns. When you have selected the veneer, you cut a piece to fill the hole. Then, you repeat the procedure with all the other elements that go to make the design—the sails, the masts, the hull, the clouds, and so on. Of course, if you continue in this manner, you will eventually finish up with a situation where just about all the base veneer has been replaced by little cutouts of contrasting veneer. When this point is reached, the resultant design can be mounted like a picture or built into something like a coffee table. Great fun!

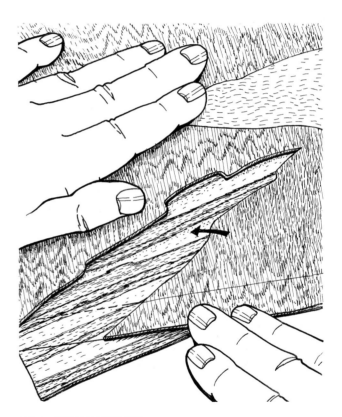

WINDOW MARQUETRY
The technique is beautifully simple and direct. All you do is cut out an element of the design and then fill it with choice veneer.

INDEX

More Great Books for Your Woodshop!

Creating Beautiful Boxes With Inlay Techniques—Now building elegant boxes is easy with this handy reference featuring 13 full-color, step-by-step projects! Thorough directions and precise drawings will have you creating beautiful inlaid boxes with features ranging from handcut dovetails to hidden compartments. #70368/$24.99/128 pages/ 230 color, 30 b&w illus./paperback

The Woodworking Handbook—Spend more time working with wood and less time shuffling through pages! This landmark reference is packed with the woodworking specifics you need to know—on topics from adhesives, design, finishing and safety to sharpening, supplies, tools and workshop math. #70371/$21.99/224 pages/199 b&w illus.

Mastering Hand Tool Techniques—Get the most from your hand tools! Over 180 tools are detailed with step-by-step instructions on how to use and care for them properly. Plus, you'll make the most of your work with tips on wood selection, precise measuring, and flawless sawing, turning, carving and joinery. #70364/$27.99/144 pages/300+ color illus.

Earn a Second Income From Your Woodworking—Turn your hobby into income with the stories of 15 professional woodworkers and the secrets they used to make their dream come true! You'll get the inside story on business planning, marketing, workshop design and tax issues to help you make the most of your dreams, too! #70377/$22.99/128 pages/ 42 b&w illus./paperback

Build Your Own Router Tables—Increase your router's accuracy, versatility and usefulness with a winning table design. Detailed plans and instructions for 3 types of tables plus a variety of specialty jigs and fixtures will help you create the right table for your shop. #70367/$21.99/160 pages/300 illus./ paperback

The Encyclopedia of Joint Making—Create the best joints for every project! This comprehensive resource shows you how to prepare lumber, prevent layout errors, select the right joint, choose the best fastener and more. #70356/$22.99/144 pages/300+ color illus.

The Woodworker's Guide to Furniture Design—Discover what it takes to design visually pleasing and comfortably functional furniture. Garth Graves shows you how to blend aesthetics and function with construction methods and material characteristics to develop designs that really work! #70355/$27.99/208 pages/110 illus.

Build Your Own Entertainment Centers—Now you can customize the construction and design of an entertainment center to fit your skill level, tools, style and budget. With this heavily illustrated guidebook, you'll explore the whole process—from selecting the wood to hardware and finishing. #70354/$22.99/128 pages/paperback

Good Wood Finishes—Take the mystery out of one of woodworking's most feared tasks! With detailed instructions and illustrations you'll learn about applying the perfect finish, preparing materials, repairing aged finishes, graining wood and much more. #70343/$19.99/128 pages/325+ color illus.

Measure Twice, Cut Once, Revised Edition—Miscalculation will be a thing of the past when you learn these effective techniques for checking and adjusting measuring tools, laying out complex measurements, fixing mistakes, making templates and much more! #70330/$22.99/144 pages/144 color illus./paperback

100 Keys to Woodshop Safety—Make your shop safer than ever with this manual designed to help you avoid potential pitfalls. Tips and illustrations demonstrate the basics of safe shopwork—from using electricity safely and avoiding trouble with hand and power tools to ridding your shop of dangerous debris and handling finishing materials. #70333/$17.99/64 pages/125 color illus.

Making Elegant Gifts From Wood—Develop your woodworking skills and make over 30 gift-quality projects at the same time! You'll find everything you're looking to create in your gifts—variety, timeless styles, pleasing proportions and imaginative designs that call for the best woods. Plus, technique sidebars and hardware installation tips make your job even easier. #70331/$24.99/128 pages/30 color, 120 b&w illus.

Getting the Very Best From Your Router— Get to know your router inside and out as you discover new jigs and fixtures to amplify its capabilities, as well as techniques to make it the most precise cutting tool in your shop. Plus, tips for comparing different routers and bits will help you buy smart for a solid long-term investment. #70328/$22.99/144 pages/ 225+ b&w illus./paperback

Good Wood Handbook, 2nd Edition—Now you can select and use the right wood for the job—before you buy. You'll discover valuable information on a wide selection of commercial softwoods and hardwoods—from common uses, color and grain to how the wood glues and takes finish. #70329/$19.99/128 pages/250 color illus.

100 Keys to Preventing & Fixing Woodworking Mistakes—Stop those mistakes before they happen—and fix those that have already occurred. Numbered tips and color illustrations show you how to work around flaws in wood; fix mistakes made with the saw, plane, router and lathe; repair badly made joints, veneering mishaps and finishing blunders; assemble projects successfully and more! #70332/$17.99/64 pages/125 color illus.

Creating Your Own Woodshop—Discover dozens of economical ways to fill unused space with the woodshop of your dreams. Charles Self shows you how to convert space, lay out the ideal woodshop, or improve your existing shop. #70229/$18.99/128 pages/162 b&w photos/illus./paperback

How To Sharpen Every Blade in Your Woodshop—You know that tools perform best when razor sharp—yet you avoid the dreaded chore. This ingenious guide brings you plans for jigs and devices that make sharpening any blade short and simple! Includes jigs for sharpening boring tools, router bits and more! #70250/$17.99/144 pages/157 b&w illus./paperback

The Woodworker's Sourcebook, 2nd Edition—Shop for woodworking supplies from home! Charles Self has compiled listings for everything from books and videos to plans and associations. Each listing has an address and telephone number and is rated in terms of quality and price. #70281/$19.99/160 pages/50 illus.